W9-ABO-954

MAHMOUD HUSSEIN is the pseudonym of Bahgat Elnadi and Adel Rifaat, French political writers of Egyptian origin. Together, they have published many successful works, including *Al-Sira, le Prophète de l'islam raconté par ses compagnons.*

MAHMOUD HUSSEIN

Understanding
the Qur'an Today

Translated by David Bond

SAQI

THE AGA KHAN UNIVERSITY
Institute for the Study of Muslim Civilisations

In memory of Khalid Muhammad Khalid
Apostle of democracy in Islam,
Our friend,
For whom faith in God was inseparable from free thought.

Published 2013 by Saqi Books
In association with the Aga Khan University Institute
for the Study of Muslim Civilisations

First published 2009 as *Penser le Coran* by Editions Grasset & Fasquelle

ISBN 978-0-86356-849-7
eISBN 978-0-86356-854-1

First published 2013 in Great Britain
Saqi Books
26 Westbourne Grove
London W2 5RH
www.saqibooks.com

A full CIP record for this book is available from the British Library.

Printed and bound by Bookwell, Finland

On the eve of 'Arafa, the Prophet implored the clemency of God for the Muslim community. God answered: "I forgive everyone, except those who have committed injustices. I must seek reparation from those who have committed injustices so that I may compensate their victims." The Prophet insisted: "Lord, You can take from Paradise what is necessary to compensate their victims and nevertheless pardon those who have committed injustices."

God did not answer.

Having arrived at Muzdalafa, the Prophet again implored him in favour of all the members of his community. This time, God consented.

Then the Prophet laughed joyfully.

—*Al Ahādīth al-Qudusiyya*

Contents

One

What the Qur'an says
and what people make it say

We were emerging from a period of several years spent writing a book which retraced the life of the Prophet Muhammad, according to the earliest Muslim chronicles.[1] Absorbed in the events of the seventh century of Arab history, we were in a sense absent from today's world, until the publication of the two volumes of the book brought us back to contemporary reality. Publication was followed by lecture tours in Europe and in some Arab countries, intended for what is usually termed "the general public". We expected that we would be questioned on the two essential themes of the Muslim chronicles: firstly, the human dimension which they restore to the figure of the Prophet, and secondly, the Qur'anic Revelation situated in its historical context. More often we spoke of other subjects. Wherever we went, people wanted first of all to know "what the Qur'an says" about elementary questions which were a source of general preoccupation.

Non-Muslims came in order to learn what they did not know. Muslims generally sought confirmation of what they thought they knew. Both groups expected simple, clear and conclusive answers – the kind of answers that we could not give them.

Can one find a Qur'anic reference to the actions of those kamikazes who blow themselves up in a public space or on the underground, indiscriminately killing combatants and civilians, young and old?

The Qur'an[2] (5:32) condemns the person who takes the life of an innocent person. The Prophet forbade Muslims to kill themselves, and permitted them to kill only armed and adult enemy combatants, excluding women, old people and children.

How can certain Muslims nevertheless commit such crimes? They quote a verse which calls for combat against the idolaters (9:3–5) and then describe as such all those whom they consider to be their enemies. They make the Qur'an say what suits them.

We find the same kind of manipulation of the text in connection with apostasy. Does the Qur'an say that apostasy incurs the death penalty? We witnessed someone defend this point of view so robustly that we began, for a moment, to doubt our own knowledge of the text. There is no such condemnation of apostasy in the Qur'an. Our interlocutor based his opinion on a verse (2:27) in which God addresses those who have violated a pact concluded with Him, warning them that they are the losers.

The stoning of adulterous women is a particularly troubling case. Numerous Muslim intellectuals continue, albeit with regret, to accept this practice on the grounds that God would have commanded it. The Qur'an, in reality, says nothing about this. This conviction lives on, supported by dubious arguments, dictated, people say, by a Qur'anic verse variously described as lost or abrogated.

What about legalised inequality between men and women, or the institution of slavery? A highly qualified woman in one of our audiences was convinced that such practices were foreign to the Qur'an. She informed us that she would accept no quotations from the Hadith (sayings of the Prophet) or the Sira (eyewitness accounts of the Prophet's companions); the Qur'an itself was the only reliable guide, in her opinion.

We began by quoting verses which permit inequality between men and women (4:34 and 2:178) and then reminded our perplexed interlocutor that we consider that the question should be seen in its historical context. The Qur'an approached the position of women in a humanitarian way, giving them rights which hitherto they had not enjoyed and accorded them, as believers, equal dignity with men, in the eyes of God. The practice of slavery was also circumscribed by moral limitations, with slave owners being advised to free as many slaves as they could, in particular in order for their sins to be pardoned. The Qur'an did not create inequalities in an existing context of equality; it brought improvements to flagrant inequalities.

A man of advanced years maintained that polygamy was a practice contrary to Islam and had been introduced long after the time of the Prophet. We were obliged to read to him, translating from Arabic, one of the Qur'anic verses which authorises a man to marry up to four wives, on the condition that he treat them equitably (4:3).

We did not expect to encounter this patchy and selective knowledge of the Qur'an, particularly among practising Muslims. We were surprised above all by the prevailing feeling among them that the Qur'an should bring clear, unequivocal and definitive answers to the questions they were asking, as it had done (or so they believed) in the case of all the questions Muslims had asked since the time of the Prophet.

Listening to one of our lectures was a young woman, her hair discreetly covered by a shawl. We were explaining the circumstances in which (according to a companion of the Prophet) the wearing of a shawl was commanded by God.

At Medina, at nightfall, women needed to leave the city in order to answer the call of nature. They were often molested by outlaws. They complained to their husbands who in turn referred the matter to the Prophet. Following these incidents the Qur'anic verse was revealed to the Prophet. By wearing a shawl, free Muslim women (not slaves) could be easily recognised and thus respected, even at night (33:59).

The young woman was visibly irritated and finally asked us how we dared believe that God, whose Book contained only eternal commandments, could have commanded the wearing of the shawl for such trivial reasons.

We replied that this episode was quoted by the most orthodox exegetes, and in any case, she was free to consider either that this verse obliged all women everywhere to wear the shawl, or that the Qur'anic text addresses a particular context which no longer exists.

Beyond the question of the tenor of particular verses, we endeavoured to underline a point that seemed obvious to us: the text of the Qur'an is closely linked to the context in which it was revealed. The series of lectures we undertook enabled us to measure the difficulty that numerous believers have in accepting this approach. Privately, they do not feel that they are allowed to accept it.

They are prevented from doing so by a doctrine which progressively took shape after the death of the Prophet and which, since then, has gravely misled many Muslims. This doctrine is based on a process of reasoning which is ostensibly unassailable. It maintains that the Qur'an, as the Word of God, transcends time, and that its verses are not linked to the context in which they were revealed. Rather, they are formulated, once and for all, to take in all possible contexts. Today, as in the past, these verses are to be accepted as they are in the text. This is a literal understanding of the text.

The believer is, therefore, faced with the following syllogism: a Muslim is a person who believes that the Qur'an is the Word of God. The person who doubts that all the verses of the Qur'an are irrevocable casts doubt on the belief that the Qur'an is the Word of God. Such a person is no longer a Muslim.

This rigid reasoning explains the difficulty in which numerous believers find themselves when they encounter Qur'anic prescriptions which they would prefer to avoid. They deceive themselves by striving to "forget" particular verses or "giving preference" to one verse over another, although they believe they have to accept that all the verses, without exception, are irrevocable.

A believer's conscience is thus troubled by a series of underlying conflicts: between fidelity to the text of the Qur'an and the pressures of reality; between timeless truth and the experience of change and relativity; and between the acceptance of arguments dictated by authority, and the exercise of personal reflection.

Certain individuals try to flee these dilemmas by embracing fundamentalism. This entails surrendering their freedom of conscience in exchange for simple certainties arbitrarily selected from the text of the Qur'an. They acknowledge reality only insofar as it seems to confirm their dogmas.

The following pages will show that these conflicts are not produced by the Qur'an, but result from a piece of misleading sophistry, according to which the Word of God must be of the same nature as God himself. As God is eternal, so too His Word must be eternal. But the Qur'an does not say this. It says the contrary. In order to become aware of this, one has to engage directly with the text of the Qur'an, abandon pre-conceived ideas and endeavour to understand the text in its context.

Such a reading of the Qur'an leads us to the three following propositions: firstly, God is not synonymous with His Word. God transcends Time, but His Word is inscribed in Time, maintaining a living link with the historical context in which God revealed it.

Secondly, the Word of God does not take on the form of a monologue but of an exchange between Heaven and Earth. God speaks, through the Prophet, with the community of the first Muslims.

Thirdly, God did not give the same weight of meaning to his Word at each moment of its Revelation. The Qur'an therefore enunciates different orders of truth, in which figure the absolute and the relative, the general and the particular, the everlasting and the transitory.

Two

The created and the uncreated

The literalist preconception was not always considered the norm. It was imposed on the Muslim community after a struggle which began following the death of the Prophet and lasted for several centuries.

In the first schools of Qur'anic interpretation there were already two opposing approaches: one which relied on the tradition received from the first generations of believers, with a commentary on the text of the Qur'an which adhered to the letter of the text, and another approach which favoured personal reflection and relied on reason.

When the first religious doctrines were outlined, a conflict developed between the Qadarites, who saw the Qur'an as underlining human free will, and the Jabrites, for whom the Qur'an gives primacy to the absolute power of God. The translation into Arabic of the Greek philosophers, and particularly the logic of Aristotle, gave added authority and coherence to the current of thought which emphasised the autonomy of reason. The great theological debate began, provoking intellectual disputations whose variety and richness are today largely forgotten. A simplified presentation of the debate identifies two main viewpoints.

The Mu'tazalites' reading of the Qur'an is characterised by confidence in the power of reason. God himself is Reason, and gave humans the ability to act freely. He will reward them at the end of time, according to their acts.

This school is opposed by the representatives of Tradition, of whom a leading member was Ibn Hanbal, founder of one of the four schools of jurisprudence. He forcefully rejected the notion of human free will, as an obstacle to the absolute power of God, which lies beyond the bounds of human reasoning.

The decisive debate took place in Baghdad in the ninth century, on the nature of the Word of God: is this Word consubstantial with God or is it only one of His attributes? Is it timeless and eternal like God, or is it distinct from Him and situated within human history?

This gave rise to the famous question concerning the status of the Qur'an: "created" or "uncreated"?

According to the Mu'tazalites, the Qur'an is "created", meaning that it is distinct from God and, unlike Him, is situated within history. Reason renders the Qur'an comprehensible to believers, who are free and responsible for their acts. They must undertake personal research to interpret the Qur'an as best they can in situations different from those in which God revealed it.

According to Ibn Hanbal the Qur'an is "uncreated". This means that it is part of the substance of God, and inseparable from Him. On the one hand the Qur'an is timeless, like God, and on the other hand, it is above reason. For believers, therefore, the intelligibility of the Qur'an's verses is less significant than the divine presence which they convey. It matters less to understand the verses than it does to absorb them more and more deeply.

The confrontation between Mu'tazalites and Hanbalites ended in the decisive victory of the latter in Baghdad towards the end of the ninth century. The debate between rationalism and traditionalism continued, employing subtle or trenchant formulations throughout the Muslim world, particularly in Andalusia.

The teachings of Ibn Taymiyya[1] in the fourteenth century, propagated by Muhammad ibn 'Abd al-Wahhab[2] in the eighteenth century, assured the victory of traditional opinion, in its narrowest and most literalist version, for centuries to come.

Throughout this period, literalism has profoundly influenced the mentality of Muslims in every area of religious science, to the extent that it seems self-evident, not even requiring comment, as though literalism were synonymous with Islam itself.

Numerous believers engage with the Qur'an as a text that should sustain their faith but not their intelligence. Reason's role is limited to grasping the primary meaning of words.

As children, they learn fragments by heart without understanding them. As adults they are familiar with the text, although they do not dare to reflect on it. They pass from one word to another, reciting or chanting the verses, and listen to extracts commented on in mosques, on television, or, perhaps, in evening classes.

The majority will not, however, embark on a personal journey in which they will discover the text. They will not search for meaning, even less for interpretation.

Depriving themselves in this way of an unhindered personal understanding of the world of the Qur'an, these believers undermine the heart of their identity and self-confidence. They tend to retreat into themselves and isolate themselves from the rest of the world, instead of launching themselves, with others, into the common adventure of human destiny.

Three

Understanding the Qur'an

The zeriba of commentary, constructed by scholars over more than a thousand years around the postulate of the uncreated Qur'an, is unlikely to be dismantled in the near future. Blocking as it does the way to a free, intelligent, and rational approach to the Qur'an, this intellectual obstacle will continue to exist as long as it is considered indispensable – which is precisely why a way around it should be found.

We propose, therefore, to engage directly with the Qur'an, trying to understand it while reading it in the light of the circumstance of its Revelation.

It is in the Qur'an that the word of God is to be found. God addresses this Word directly and to each believer in person, who has to make the required effort to read, understand, listen to and draw inspiration from the Word throughout his or her life on earth. This is the first duty of believers.

Islam gave a name in former times to this exercise of direct and responsible reading: ijtihad, or the constant effort that each person is called to make in the service of the Word of God.

It is notoriously difficult to engage with the text of the Qur'an. There is no guarantee that readers will understand it, mainly because the 6,236 verses comprising the Qur'an were gathered in one book twenty years after the death of the Prophet and arranged in an unexplained manner depicting neither their chronology, nor the various circumstances in which they were revealed.

The defenders of a literalist approach have exploited this difficulty in reading the Qur'an to justify the necessary interposition of their commentaries between the reader and the text. How can one approach the text without them?

A solution exists; one that goes back to the experience of the companions of the Prophet. The majority of them did not immediately grasp the meaning of the verses that the Prophet recited to them. They went to see him, individually or in groups, and questioned him. He answered by clarifying, commenting and illustrating the different verses.

After his death, it was his companions' task to pass on to an ever-growing number of believers the words of the

Prophet, enriched by what the companions could remember of the time and place in which the verses were revealed to him.

Some generations after the death of the last surviving companions, collectors of traditions relating to the Prophet and chroniclers began to assemble this mass of eyewitness reports, initially handed down orally, and gradually written down.

Based on these reports, an essential instrument for understanding the text of the Qur'an came into being: the study of the context of the Revelation of verses, a study which gradually became a fully fledged branch of Qur'anic commentary.

This instrument is indispensable for whosoever wishes today to engage directly with the text of the Qur'an. It is a compass which helps the reader to progress in his or her understanding of the text.

When this kind of reading is undertaken under the guidance of faith and intelligence, it is sufficient to refute the doctrine of the "uncreated Qur'an". That the Qur'an is a form of transcendence revealed in time is a truth that is evident to reason.

Four

The historical setting for Revelation

Let us briefly recall the historical setting in which the Qur'an was revealed.

At the turn of the seventh century, the immense territories of the Arabian Peninsula were inhabited by nomadic or semi-nomadic tribes. A small number became sedentary, settling in a few towns, mostly in the south, in the fertile region of Yemen, or in western central areas along the Red Sea. Mecca, in contrast to other centres of population, possessed three distinctive geographical, economic and religious features.

Surrounded on all sides by overhanging mountains, Mecca is protected by its natural setting. The city benefited from this in order to become the crossroads for caravan routes linking Yemen to Syria and Iraq. It took a month by camel to travel to Mecca from Damascus in the north or Aden in the south, and twenty-five days from Basra in the east.

In addition, Mecca was the site of a sanctuary known as the Kaaba, venerated in many parts of the Peninsula.

The Kaaba contained the idols of the Meccan pantheon as well as those of numerous tribes outside the city. During the regular pilgrimage periods, all these tribes observed a truce and met in Mecca to venerate their divinities, exchange news and goods, and negotiate or re-negotiate alliances.

Historians of the time agree that the large tribes inhabiting the centre of the Peninsula were fiercely independent in spirit. They were thus able to stave off concurrent attempts by Persia and Byzantium to integrate the central region into their zone of influence. There are reports that Alexander the Great, on his way to Persia, had planned to occupy the centre of Arabia, a plan he subsequently had to abandon.

The same spirit of independence led these polytheist tribes to resist the attraction of Judaism and Christianity. Jewish and Christian communities, although small minorities, had settled in a few towns: Yathrib and Khaybar in the case of the former, Najran in the latter. The Arabs halted there each time they followed the trade routes between Mecca and Damascus in the north or between Mecca and Yemen in the south. They debated with both

Jews and Christians, although conversions were very rare.

Nevertheless, certain polytheists displayed a real interest in monotheism at this period. They sought a unified vision of the things of this world and the world to come, but were unable to formulate the principles of such a vision. They refused, however, to adopt those proposed by the Jews and the Christians, as their Scriptures contained references too far removed from Arab culture. Moreover, the Jews were protected by Persia and the Christians by Byzantium.

According to scholars of the time, at the end of the sixth century, a mysterious rumour circulated that an Arab prophet would arrive. A famous poet aspired in vain to this role, while several individuals belonging to various polytheist tribes claimed to be inspired by the one true God.

Five

The beginnings of Revelation

Muhammad ibn 'Abd Allah ibn 'Abd al-Muttalib was born in Mecca, in the year 570, in the prestigious yet impoverished clan of the Banu 'Abd al-Muttalib, traditional guardians of the sanctuary of the Kaaba.

He grew up as an orphan, his father having died shortly before his birth, and his mother when he was six years old. Initially, Muhammad was looked after by his grandfather, then, after his death, by the oldest of his paternal uncles. His childhood and adolescence were doubtless marked by material poverty.

Little is known of the first forty years of his life. The essential elements of what we do know derive from what Muhammad himself later recounted to his companions.

Muhammad's spiritual temperament led him at certain seasons to seek periods of solitude. Intellectually precocious, he sought out the custodians of learning, particularly

Christians, whom he generally met during caravan journeys. Muhammad's upright character and his probity were recognised, and people naturally trusted him.

At the age of twenty-five he attracted the attention of Khadija, a wealthy businesswoman, fifteen years his senior and already widowed. She made it known to him that he could ask for her hand in marriage. She remained his only wife until her death, affording him support and constant encouragement in the tribulations that he encountered.

Around the year 610, according to one traditional account, Muhammad was meditating in a cave situated on the hill of Hira, not far from Mecca. A mysterious encounter took place during which Muhammad learned that God had chosen him as his final Messenger. Subsequently, and throughout his life, Muhammad continued to receive intermittently the Word of God.

The Revelation was experienced by the Prophet as a manifestation of an absolute entity, the expression of a will outside his own conscience, a will that imposed itself through the overwhelming significance of the truth it communicated.

The traditional accounts of the circumstances in which the Revelation began include a number of variants.

Gabriel came to me while I was sleeping. He held a piece of brocade on which there was writing and said to me:
– Read.
I said:

– I do not know how to read. I have never read and I do not know how to read. I can neither read nor write.

Gabriel pressed me, so strongly that I thought that death was approaching, then he released me and said:

– Read.

I said:

– What shall I read? I see nothing to read and I can neither read nor write.

I only spoke in this way to avoid Gabriel inflicting on me for a second time what he had inflicted on me. Then he said:

– **Recite, in the name of your Lord! He who created! He created man from a blood clot. Recite! Your Lord is most bountiful. He taught with the pen. He taught man what he knew not.**

I read after him and he finally left me. I woke up with a start. It was as though his words had been engraved on my heart. (...)

The poet or the person possessed is the most hateful of God's creatures in my eyes. I cannot bear even their sight. I said to myself: 'Has Muhammad ibn 'Abd Allah become a poet or a man possessed?' No, people will not take me for either. I shall throw myself from a great height. I shall kill myself and be delivered.'

I went out with this intention but half way to my destination I heard a voice from heaven saying:

– Muhammad, you are the Messenger of God and I am Gabriel.

I looked up towards the heavens and saw Gabriel, in

the form of a man whose feet barred the horizon. He was saying to me:

– Muhammad, you are the Messenger of God and I am Gabriel.

I stopped to look at him, forgetting what I had resolved to do, going neither forwards nor backwards. Then I tried to look away, but wherever I looked I saw him, covering the horizon. I remained motionless, going neither forwards nor backwards, for such a long time that Khadija sent people to look for me; they went as far as Mecca and came back, while I remained immobile.

Then Gabriel left me and I returned home.

(Qur'an, 96:1–5) (Ibn Ishaq)[1]

The Messenger of God was on the hill of Ajyad, when he saw, far off in the heavens, an angel seated cross-legged, who cried out:

– O Muhammad, I am Gabriel! O Muhammad, I am Gabriel.

The Messenger of God panicked. He saw him every time he raised his eyes towards the heavens. He returned hurriedly towards Khadija, informed her of what had happened, and said:

– Khadija, in God's name, there is nothing I detest more than these idols and these fortune-tellers ... I see light, I hear noises ... I fear that I have become one of these fortune-tellers or that I am possessed by a djinn.

(Ibn Sa'd)[2]

According to 'A'isha, who became one of the Prophet's wives after the death of Khadija, the beginning of things went back to an earlier period.

The first signs of the Revelation for the Messenger of God were authentic visions, which he had at the first light of morning. God inspired him with a love of solitude. He spent time alone in the cave of Hira'. He was accustomed to meditate there for a certain number of nights, then, having returned home, he collected provisions and left again for the cave. It is there that Truth surprised him, with these words:

– O Muhammad, you are the Messenger of God.

The Messenger of God recounts what happened next:

I fell on my knees, then dragged myself, trembling, to where Khadija was and said:

– Cover me, cover me!

The fear left me. Then 'he' came back and said to me:

– O Muhammad, you are the Messenger of God.

I thought of throwing myself from a cliff. As soon as this thought occurred to me, he appeared to me and said:

– O Muhammad, I am Gabriel and you are the Messenger of God.

Then he said:

– Read.

I answered:

– I cannot read.

He drew me close to him three times, until my strength
ebbed away.

Then he said:

**– Recite, in the name of your Lord! He who created!
He created man from a blood clot.**

(96:1–2) (Al-Tabari)[3]

Certain companions of the Prophet later introduced
doubts about the first verses of Revelation, which they
claim did not commence by the words "Recite: In the
Name of thy Lord ..." and were not situated in the context
described above.

According to them, the Prophet said to his entourage:

– Cover me! Cover me!

Then these verses were revealed to him:

**You who are enfolded in your garments: Stand up
and warn! Magnify your Lord! Purify your garments!
And abandon impurity!**

(74:1–5) (al-Wahidi)[4] (al-Mawardi)[5]

It is not conclusively determined whether the Revelation
began at Hira or at Ajyad, whether Muhammad was asleep
or awake, or if the Word made itself heard directly or
through Gabriel; in the latter case it is not clear whether
the angel manifested himself visibly or only audibly.

Subsequently Gabriel would come to see the Prophet

on numerous occasions in a form that only the Prophet could perceive. More rarely, Gabriel appeared to everyone, but in a human aspect.

Revelation for the most part could occur without the involvement of Gabriel and could take place without him. It came upon the Prophet without an intermediary and without a verbal form.

Al Harith ibn Hisham, companion of the Prophet, asked him one day, towards the end of his life, how he received the Revelation. He got this reply:

– Sometimes it is like the ringing of a bell, ringing which reaches its fullest volume before becoming quieter when I have grasped its meaning. Sometimes the angel takes human form, he speaks to me, and I grasp the meaning of what he says.

On another occasion, the Prophet says:

– Revelation reaches me in two ways. It is brought by Gabriel, who passes it on to me in the same way as men speak to one another. This may elude me. Or revelation reaches me in the same way as the ringing of a bell which penetrates my heart. This remains with me.

(Ibn Sa'd)[6]

The two Hadith concur on the two ways in which Revelation can be communicated. The second Hadith adds an observation of great importance: it is the non-verbal form of revelation, penetrating directly the heart of the Prophet like the ringing of a bell that remains indelibly inscribed in the memory of the Prophet.

ભ

Shortly after the initial revelation received by the Prophet, the Revelation ceased. The interruption was so long that the Prophet was worried and wondered whether he had had a hallucination or whether God was angry with him because he was afraid, or because he had thought of putting an end to his life.

> Khadija finally said to her husband:
> – It is as though your God has abandoned you!
> (Al-Wahidi)[7]

But Revelation recommenced and God reassured his Prophet, discounting the speculation of Khadija: **Your Lord has not abandoned you, nor disdains!** (93:3). The Word of God is revealed to the Prophet in the form of verses (paragraphs), of unequal length, which later would be regrouped into suras (chapters). In Arabic, the literal expression is that Revelation "comes down" or that God "makes revelation descend" on the Prophet.

The Prophet began by reciting the verses he received to a small group of people to whom he was close: his wife

Khadija, his cousin 'Ali, his adopted son Zayd, and his friend Abu Bakr. He recommended to those who embraced the new faith to keep this secret for the time being. Aware of how foreign the faith of the incipient community was to the beliefs and customs of the inhabitants of Mecca, he waited until his fellow-Muslims were sufficiently numerous before openly proclaiming the new religion.

God however commanded Muhammad to break his silence: **Warn your closest relatives** (26:214).

The Prophet understood by this that he must openly call the people of his clan to the religion of God. He was unable to make up his mind and went as far as to remain in his home for a month. God insisted, in a more threatening manner.

According to 'Ali ibn Abu Talib:

When the verse 'Warn your closest relatives' was revealed to the Prophet, he said to me:

– 'Ali, God has ordered me to warn my kinsfolk. This troubles me for I know that if I insist, they will behave in a detestable manner. I pretended not to hear, but Gabriel came and said to me: 'Muhammad, if you do not do what you have been ordered to do. God will punish you!

Acting against his own inclinations, the Prophet obeyed. He assembled in his home the men of his clan to whom he announced:

– By the One God who has no associates, I am the Messenger of God. He sent me to you in particular and to all people in general ... by God, you will die in the same way as you sleep and you will come back to life as you awake from sleep. You will answer for your deeds. You will receive good for the good you have done and evil for the evil you have done. It will be eternal Paradise or eternal Hell.

(Al-Dhahabi)[8]

Six

The Qur'an in its historical context

The Revelation of the Qur'an began around 610 and ended in 632 with the death of the Prophet Muhammad. This period is divided into two sub-periods, distinct in space and time.

Firstly, for a period of twelve years, there were the revelations at Mecca. Then, from 622, for a period of ten years, there were the revelations which took place at Yathrib, renamed Medina after the death of the Prophet. These periods appear in the text of the Qur'an, in which all the verses are situated in Mecca or Medina.

A number of Qur'anic themes are present in both periods, although there are certain basic characteristic themes particular to one or other of the periods. The difference in themes is a consequence of the different contexts of Mecca and Medina.

During the Meccan period, believers were very few in

number. Their total number was no more than around a hundred. United by their common faith, they did not constitute, in daily life, a distinct community. They continued to live individually with their clans, in their respective families, even though they were more and more ill at ease, and treated intolerantly.

The Word which the Prophet passed on to them, and which transformed them into a cohesive community around him, was centred on the main principles – metaphysical, eschatological, ritual – of the new religion. In other words, the vertical relationship between believers and God.

God is unique, all-powerful and compassionate. Muhammad is His messenger. Human beings are called, during their earthly existence, to bear witness to the unique oneness of God, to the unity of His creation and to the finality of life itself, the return to God, whence it comes.

People are personally responsible before God for their acts. They will account for their actions at the Last Judgement, when they will be individually rewarded or punished, for all eternity.

While they were in Mecca, the Muslims, scattered among their kinsfolk, did not have to deal with the challenges inherent to a distinct, autonomous community.

It was in Yathrib, from 622 onwards, the year of the Hegira (from hijra, meaning "emigration"), that they began to form a community of faith and life, where spirituality inspired the organisation of daily life.

The Muhajirun (or emigrants, who come from Mecca), the Ansars (or "supporters", inhabitants of Yathrib who welcomed the Muslims into their homes) and the new arrivals who joined them gradually from all the tribes of Arabia, formed a pluralistic community, with tribal differences as well as social disparities. They also had to learn to define themselves as Muslims, in the face of other religions and, within a short space of time, to resist the external threat of tribal coalitions.

They waited for God to teach them how to live, both among themselves and in relation to others, guiding them in the earthly relations that structure human interaction.

Why did the Qur'an not deal with these questions at Mecca? Why did it only start to deal with them at Yathrib?

The answer is that these questions had not yet come to the forefront in Mecca and would only begin to do so at Yathrib.

Before examining, one by one, the main themes reflecting the link between the text and its historical context, we need to evoke a wider time-framework in which the Qur'an is situated: the history of Creation itself.

Seven

The Qur'an in the time of Creation

Through numerous verses of the Qur'an, in particular those that God devoted to the deeds of the prophets who preceded Muhammad on the earth, a Qur'anic narrative takes form. It expresses the unity and coherence of the design that God pursues in his creation. This develops, in a series of cycles, from Genesis to the Last Judgement, culminating in eternal life. At various periods in this unfolding history, God sent a prophet with the mission of communicating His Word to people, sometimes in the form of a Book. Muhammad was the last of these prophets, and the Qur'an was the last of these books.

Having decreed the creation of the universe, which took six days, God deployed His power and majesty:

Your Lord is God Who created the heavens and the earth in six days, then settled firmly on the throne, to order the world's affairs.

(Qur'an, 10:3)

43

The first human being appeared at the end of the sixth day:

> **Remember when your Lord said to the angels: "I shall create a human being from dry clay, from fetid mud. When I give him the proper shape and breathe into him from My spirit, you are to fall down prostrate before him."**
>
> (15:28–9)

The Qur'an calls on people to recognise the signs that God has placed on their path on earth to guide them back to Him. Everything comes from God and everything leads back to Him:

> **Say: "We belong to God, and to him we shall return."**
>
> (2:156)

In these signs, people are invited to perceive that God is one, that He is mighty and compassionate:

> **In the creation of the heavens and the earth,**
> **In the cycle of night and day,**
> **In ships that plough the sea, to mankind's benefit,**
> **In what God causes to descend from the sky of water,**
> **Giving life to the earth, hitherto dead,**
> **And peopling it with all manner of crawling creatures,**
> **In varying the winds and clouds, which run their course between sky and earth –**

In these are signs of people who reflect.

(2:164)

But people are constantly tempted by evil. Thus, at different places and times, they forget God, which always leads to one form or another of idol-worship. God is wrathful, He sanctions, He punishes. But more often, He pardons:

And fear God, for God is All-Pardoning,
Compassionate to each.

(49:12)

From time to time, He offers humans an exceptional chance for salvation, sending them a new prophet, a bearer of his Message, always the same but in varying forms and languages. This message is that of the "true religion", of "abandon to God"; in Arabic, *islam*. In this sense, all the prophets of God are Muslims.

Some of them were bearers of Books. These Books are different forms of the same book, whose formless essence is that designated by the Qur'an as Umm al Kitab, the archetype, the original Book.

For every matter decided there is a Register:
God erases what He will, and ratifies.
With Him is the Archetype of the Book.

(13:38–9)

Abraham, Moses and Jesus are among the greatest of the prophets. They accomplished their mission. But after their death the Message they brought was betrayed and the books revealed to Moses and Jesus were altered. Then God decided to send Muhammad, who would be His last Messenger, bearer of the Book in its final form:

This is a Book We have sent down, blessed, and confirming previous revelations ...

(6:92)

(One may note the continuity of meaning between the signs that God places in the world to reveal His presence to humans, and the signs that He places in His Book in which He reveals his Word: the same word in Arabic, aya, designates the signs of God's work of creation and the verses of the Qur'an.)

The Qur'an reveals a succession of supernatural and exceptional events which punctuate the designs of divine providence: the periodic return of prophets, whose mission it is to announce His Word to humans who constantly forget it.

This narrative makes it impossible to reduce the Qur'an to a sort of collage of divine truths without any chronology, to be read in no particular order. Some events preceded others – the Torah precedes the Gospel, which in its turn precedes the Qur'an, and certain prophetic

figures appear before others – Abraham, Mos₊
Muhammad follow one another in this order.

Through this succession of supernatural eve.
Qur'anic narrative highlights how, within the ᴄ ᴧll
divine plan of creation, God intervenes directly in history
each time that He judges it necessary, creating a supernatural and exceptional event: the revelation of His Word to
a prophet whose mission is to offer humans a new chance
of salvation. This notion is also central to the twenty-two-
year long period of the Revelation of the Qur'an.

Eight

Text and context

The Qur'an, we noted earlier, reveals itself to the person who engages with the text without preconceived ideas, and makes an effort to understand it, placing it in the context of the event of revelation.

In this spirit, we shall present several series of verses, arranged around the principal challenges that the Prophet and his companions had to confront. God intervened to reveal to them the path to follow in connection with these challenges.

The verses are preceded by sayings of the Prophet, or by eyewitness accounts of his companions, without which the meaning of the verses would be difficult to grasp, sometimes even incomprehensible. The sayings of the Prophet and accounts of his companions are taken from the principal books of exegesis dealing with the circumstances of Revelation. A few words on the history of these books are necessary.

CR

Arabia at the beginning of the seventh century was a society with an oral tradition. In Mecca at this time there seem to have been no more than twenty people able to read and write. The Prophet left no written document and the various circumstances in which he received the Revelation of the verses of the Qur'an are known to us only by the accounts of his contemporaries. They recounted the words of the Prophet as well as the events they witnessed.

One of the close companions of the Prophet, 'Abd Allah ibn Mas'ud, considered himself authorised to say: "There is not a single sura of the Book of God of which I do not know its place of revelation, not a single sura of the Book of God of which I do not know the reason for its revelation."[1]

But the various eyewitness reports do not always exactly concur. They contain variants more or less different from one another. They are sometimes contradictory: a companion of the Prophet can recall an event, associating with it verses that another will associate with an earlier or a later event.

In some cases it is not possible to know for sure whether certain verses belong to the Meccan period (the first twelve years of Revelation) or the Medinan period (the last ten years).

In addition, these accounts were only written down

much later. They were transmitted by word of mouth, then from one generation to another, and transcribed in fragmentary form using improvised material. Starting in the ninth century, these accounts were gathered together and set down on paper – that is to say nearly two centuries after the end of Revelation.

They were collected, selected and verified, thanks to the patient labour of tradition specialists (working in particular on the Hadith, or sayings of the Prophet) or chroniclers who worked on the Sira, eyewitness accounts of the companions of the Prophet. All these scholars spent years reconstructing records of transmission going back, step by step, to those who had seen the Prophet in person.

The reliability of the details recorded has been reduced by the passage of time, by the material conditions of the transmission of the accounts and sometimes by a religious or political bias on the part of scholars involved. From a historical point of view, a number of questions thus remain unanswered.

The mere existence of the tradition specialists' and chroniclers' work is already a blessing since it is our only link with the period which saw the beginning of Islam. Cross-checking, comparisons, and inspired guesswork are certainly required of researchers.

But it is important to emphasise that in the domain of religion, Qur'anic commentary was able to develop only on the basis of these reports and eyewitness accounts.

All the commentaries link the verses to the circumstances of their "descent". The first work exclusively concerned with this link is the eleventh-century Asbab al Nuzul ("Circumstances of the descent of the Qur'an") by al-Wahidi.

All the works devoted to this particular aspect of exegesis have subsequently been called Asbab al Nuzul. Among the most famous authors are Al-Dahhak, Muqatil, Ibn Ishaq, Al-Waqidi, Ibn Sa'd, Al-Tabari and Al-Baladhuri. We shall refer to all of these works, and not merely the book of al-Wahidi, when quoting from sources related to Asbab al Nuzul.

Today's readers have at their disposal, therefore, a number of key sources which open up numerous fields of research and reflection.

Based on our own selection of examples, the following pages highlight the vital and varied relationship of the Qur'anic text with the context in which it was revealed.

Nine

God replies to the arguments
of the polytheists

On hearing the message of the Prophet, the Meccans were amazed. Bereft of any metaphysical or eschatological vision, they lived in a world hemmed in by dark and anarchic forces. The only milestones in the past were the mythical deeds and exploits of their ancestors. The stone idols venerated by the tribes of Mecca were the only sources of protection.

The notion of one, all-powerful God, who orders the affairs of the world, before whom each person is called upon to personally account for their acts, seemed to them bizarre and dangerous.

Although the majority of the Meccans rejected the message, they did not combat it immediately. Paradoxically, for a time the clan structure of society, albeit challenged by Islam, protected the Prophet.

As long as his paternal uncle, Abu Talib, clan chief of the Banu Hashim, who had brought up the young Muhammad, extended his protection to the Prophet, all the members of the clan defended Muhammad as one man. The other clans knew that if they attacked the Prophet they would be attacking the whole clan as well as its possible allies.

The importance of this clan kinship can be appreciated if one remembers that Abu Talib offered this protection to his nephew while he, and the great majority of the members of his clan, were faithful to the paganism of their ancestors and were unreceptive to the message of Islam.

The Meccan members of other clans began by mocking Muhammad or by questioning him ironically. They only became openly hostile when he directly attacked the cult of their ancestors and their idols. After the death of his uncle, and when the protection of Muhammad by the clan of the Banu Hashim was no longer assured, they fought against him.

Having been for a long period unanimously esteemed and respected, Muhammad was distressed by the mounting disaffection displayed towards him:

Some Meccans said to the Prophet:
– Renouncing our religion will bring misfortune upon you!
God then revealed these verses:

We did not bring down the Qur'an upon you to make you suffer; rather, it is a Remembrance to him who fears God. It is a revelation from Him Who created the earth and highest heavens.

(Qur'an, 20:2–4) (Al Zamakhshari)[1] (Al Wahidi)[2]

Meccans came and said to the Messenger of God:

– Describe your God to us. Tell us. What is he made of? Of what metal? Gold, brass, or silver? Does he eat or drink? From whom did he inherit the world? To whom will he leave it as a legacy?

God revealed this reply:

Say: "He is God, Unique,
God, Lord Supreme!
Neither begetting nor begotten,
And none can be His peer."

(112:1–4) (Al-Wahidi)[3]

These Meccans said again:

– Why was this Book not revealed all at once, in the same way as the other Books? After which God revealed these verses:

Those who blaspheme say: "If only the Qur'an had been sent down upon him whole and undivided!"
Rather, to confirm your heart with it! And We made it to be chanted, a sublime chant!

(25:32) (Al Zamakhshari)[4]

This verse underlines that the Qur'an "descended" over a period of time because God wished to strengthen the heart of Muhammad: a human person, his humanity being subject to the dimension of time.

The refusal of the Qur'an by the Meccans was a bitter blow to the Prophet who had hitherto been accustomed to his entourage believing what he said. His worst enemy, Abu Jahl [chief of a rival clan] said to him:

– It is not you that we reject, as we know that you are sincere, it is the words that you recite to us!

So God revealed:

We know you are grieved by what they say. It is not you they call the lie to, but the signs of God that the wrongdoer abjures.

(6:33) (Al Zamakhshari)[5]

The Prophet had received threats [from other opposing clans] and his uncle Abu Talib feared for his life. He decided to protect him by having him accompanied in all his journeys by men of their clan, the Banu Hashim. [The consequence was that the journeys of the Prophet were limited.]

God intervened to put an end to this practice:

God shall protect you from mankind.

The Prophet refused the protection offered by his uncle, saying:

– Uncle, all-powerful God protects me from men and from djinns.

(5:67) (Al Wahidi)[6]

When the uncle of the Prophet, Abu Talib, fell seriously ill, certain notables of rival clans saw an opportunity to sow distrust between the uncle and the nephew. They said to Abu Talib:

– Ask Muhammad to bring you something that can cure you from this Paradise that he is always talking about.

Abu Talib sent one of them to look for the Messenger of God who was at the Mosque with Abu Bakr. The man said:

– O Muhammad, your uncle has this message for you: I am old, weak, and unwell. Bring me from this Paradise that you are speaking about some food or drink that will heal me.

Abu Bakr interrupted:

– The all-powerful God has forbidden this food to the infidels.

The man returned to Abu Talib and said:

– I passed your message on to Muhammad. He said nothing, but Abu Bakr, who was beside him, said: the all-powerful God has forbidden this food to the infidels.

Abu Talib sent another man, with the same message, to the Messenger of God who, this time, answered himself:

– God has forbidden the infidels all food and drink that comes from Paradise.

Then the Messenger of God decided to go and see Abu Talib. He sat down beside him and said:

– Uncle, may you be rewarded for all you have done for me. You brought me up and then you protected me. Say a word, only one, so that I can plead your cause before God on the Day of Judgement.

– What is this word, nephew?

– Say: there is no god but God with whom no-one is associated.

– You have always advised me well. By God, if I did not fear that Quraysh[7] would say that I trembled in the face of death, I would do that for you!

His family cried:

– O Abu Talib, you are the senior member of the religion of our ancestors ...

Then Abu Talib said to his nephew:

– The women of Quraysh must not be able to say that your uncle trembled in the face of death.

The Messenger of God replied:

– I shall not cease to ask the pardon of God for you, unless he forbid me to do this.

So after Abu Talib died the Messenger of God implored the all-powerful God to pardon his uncle.[8] Then the Muslims said to one another:

– What is to stop us in our turn imploring the pardon of God for our own parents? Abraham did this for his father and Muhammad for his uncle ...

They began to implore the pardon of God for their ancestors, who like Abu Talib, had died without embracing Islam.

Then God revealed this verse:

It is not right for the Prophet and the believers to ask forgiveness for polytheists, even if they are relatives, once it has become clear to them that they are denizens of hell.

(9:113) (Al Wahidi)[9]

The polytheists tried a new manoeuvre against the Prophet. He had presented the Qur'an as a Book of God, revealed in the wake of the Torah and the Gospel, and some of his Meccan enemies thought they could induce the Jews of Yathrib to bring to bear new, carefully honed arguments against him.

They said to themselves:

– Why do two of us not go to Yathrib to ask the Jewish scholars what they think of Muhammad and his claims?

Two envoys were entrusted with this mission, and were told:

– Describe Muhammad to the Jewish scholars, quote his words to them and question them. Their knowledge of the prophets is greater than ours.

When the two envoys arrived in Yathrib, they said to the Jewish scholars:

– You are people of the Torah; we would like to know what you think about this man and his doings.

The Jewish scholars replied:

– Ask him three questions. Question him firstly about the surprising adventure of a group of young people who disappeared at the beginning of time. Then, ask him about a traveller who crossed the Earth from East to West. He should tell you who he is and what his position is. Question him finally about the Spirit. He should tell you what it is. If he answers these three questions, follow him. He is a prophet, a messenger of God. If he does not answer, he is an imposter. You shall decide his fate.

The envoys of Quraysh went and asked these three questions to the Messenger of God, who said to them:

– I shall answer you tomorrow.

But he omitted to say: 'If God wills.'

He stayed in his home for two weeks, without receiving a Revelation from God or Gabriel coming to see him. The Messenger of God was even more distressed as the people of Quraysh began to become impatient and say: he said to us tomorrow and for two weeks he has avoided answering our questions!

Then Gabriel appeared. The Messenger of God said to him:

– O Gabriel, you absented yourself for such a long time that I have had some doubts ...

Gabriel communicated to him the Word of God:

And do not say of anything, "I shall do this tomorrow" unless you add: "If God wills."

Then he dictated the response of God to the three questions that had been asked.

(The group of young people who had disappeared were the "People of the Cave" who wanted to flee their idolatrous community, so as to adore the one, true God. They took refuge in a cave, where God kept them asleep for three centuries, before bringing them back to life as a reminder, by this miracle, of his presence among their people.)

Nevertheless, we divulged their presence, that they might know that God's promise is true and that the Hour shall come, no doubt about it.

(The traveller who crossed the earth from East to West is "the two-horned" Dhu'l Qarnayn, whom some suggest was none other than Alexander the Great.)

They ask you about the two-horned, Dhu'l Qarnayn.
Say: "I shall recite to you some mention of him." We had established him firmly on earth, and granted him a path to the knowledge of all things.

(On the Spirit:)

They ask you about the soul.
Say: "The soul belongs to the realm of my Lord, and of knowledge you have been granted but little."

(18:23–4, 21, 83–4; 17:85) (Ibn Ishaq)

61

One evening, having met behind the Kaaba, certain notables of Quraysh had a message brought to Muhammad:

– The leaders of your people have met in order to speak to you. Come to see them.

He went to see them, hoping that they were beginning to change their position with regard to Islam. But when he sat down among them, they said to him:

– Nephew, you are one of us. You have a distinguished position in your clan and your lineage. However, you do great wrong to your people. You have fractured their unity and decried their dreams, you have spoken ill of their gods and their religion, you have calumnied [harmed the reputation of] their ancestors. If, by your message you seek riches, we shall give you some of our wealth, so that you may be the richest among us. If it is rank that you seek, we shall make you our leader and we shall solve no dispute without you. If you seek the throne, we shall make you our king. If you are in the end unable to shake off these visions which come to you from the jinns, we shall make available the necessary resources to care for you and cure you.

The Messenger of God answered: I have no interest in what you offer me. I do not come to you seeking wealth, power or royalty. God designated me as his messenger among you. He revealed His Book to me and ordered me to bring you good news and warnings. I have communicated to you the Message of my Lord and I have given you advice. If you accept this Message, it will be for your good, on earth as in the world to come. Should you reject it, I shall have only to wait the decree of God, who will settle matters definitively between us.

– If you accept none of our suggestions, recognise that our country is the most inhospitable there is, where water is rarer and life harder than anywhere else. Ask your God, then, to come to our aid, to push back these hills which hem us in, to extend our domains, make rivers flow like those of Syria and Iraq. Ask him too to bring back to life some of our ancestors, among them our common ancestor, Qusayy, who was a man of truth. We shall question them about your message and we shall ask them to say if you speak truth or error. If you can accomplish this and our ancestors vouch for you, we shall know in what esteem God holds you and that you are truly his messenger, as you say.

– God did not send me to you for this. He merely gave me the task of transmitting to you His message and I have done so.

– If you can accomplish nothing for us, then accomplish this for yourself: ask your God to send an angel to confirm what you are saying and be a reference for us. Ask him too to reward you with gardens and palaces, to send you gold and silver, to spare you the efforts that we see you making in the market places, to earn your living. Let him accomplish this and then we shall know the rank you occupy in the eyes of your God and that you are truly his messenger.

– No, I ask my Lord nothing of the kind.

– Well then, order the sky to fall on our heads, since you claim that God can do anything. We shall believe in you only if we see this.

– That depends on God's will alone. If He wills it, it will come to pass.

One of them added:

– By God, I shall never believe in you. Unless you take a ladder to climb up before me into the heavens, to re-descend with four angels who will confirm everything you say to us ...

The Prophet left them, deeply saddened. He had wanted to believe, on receiving their invitation, that they were beginning to come closer to him. He realised that in reality they had become more and more distant from him.

God addressed him at two moments. Firstly, He took up the challenges made by Quraysh:

They say: "We will not trust you unless you cause a spring to gush forth for us from the ground; or else you come to own a garden of palm trees and vines, and you cause rivers to gush forth in torrents through it all; or you make the sky fall upon us in bits and pieces, as you allege; or you summon God and the angels in our presence; or else you come to own a house made of gold; or you ascend to the sky – nor will we trust your ascent unless you bring down upon us a book we can read."

Secondly, God dictated to Muhammad the reply he was to make.

Say: "Glory be to my Lord! Am I anything other than a human being, a Messenger?"

Nothing prevented mankind from believing, when Guidance came to them, except their saying, "Did God really send a mere human as Messenger?"

Say: "Had earth been peopled by angels, walking about, their minds at ease, We would have sent down upon them from heaven an angel as messenger."

Say: "Let God suffice as witness between me and you – with His worshippers He is All-Versed, All-Seeing."

He whom God guides is truly guided; he whom He leads astray, for him you shall find no protectors apart from Him. We shall herd them, tumbled upon their faces, on the Day of Resurrection – blind, dumb and deaf. Their refuge will be hell; whenever its flames subside, We intensify the blaze upon them.

(17:90–7) (Ibn Ishaq)[11]

There were in Mecca two Christian slaves of Byzantine origin. They were reading aloud from books in their language. The Prophet, passing by, heard them. This sufficed for the polytheists to accuse him of re-employing their words in what he claimed was a Book revealed to him. God caused the following verses to descend:

We know that they say: "A mere human is teaching him."

The speech of him to whom they allude is foreign, but this is clear Arabic speech.

(16:103) (Al-Zamakhshari)[12]

God refers here to a specific event, to particular people, and to a precise dispute.

Some men from Quraysh came to the Messenger of God and said:

– O Muhammad you have told us that Moses has a baton, with which he has split a rock in order to cause twelve springs to burst forth; and that Jesus raised the dead to life; and that Salih brought the camel that the people of Thamūd had asked for. Perform some miracles like those for us and we shall believe you!

The Messenger of God asked them:

– What kind of miracle would you have me do?

– Let Mount al-Safā change into gold!

– And if I do so, will you believe me?

– Yes, by God, we shall all believe you, if you do it.

The Messenger of God asked almighty God that this miracle be accomplished. Gabriel visited him and said to him:

– When almighty God commands that a miracle take place and afterwards people remain unbelievers, the punishment of God is terrible. He destroys them. It is better for these people to remain unbelievers until those of them who are going to repent finally do so.

The Messenger of God said:

– Let them remain in unbelief, until those of them who are going to repent finally do so.

Then God revealed these verses:

They swear by God the mightiest oath that if a miracle is performed before them they would believe in it.

Say: "Miracles can only come from God." But how do you know? It may be that even if a miracle is performed before them they would still not believe.

(6:109) (Ibn Kathir)[13]

Men of Quraysh said to the Messenger of God :

– We have questioned the Jews of Yathrib about you. They have said that they did not recognise you. Find someone to bear witness that it is God who sends you to us as his Messenger.

God revealed this reply:

But God bears witness to what He revealed to you. He revealed it with His knowledge. And the angels bear witness. And God suffices as witness.

(4:166) (Maqatil)[14]

They said to the Messenger of God:

– We are linked by bonds of kinship. Tell us, therefore, when the Hour must come.

God revealed the reply:

They ask you about the Hour and when it will alight.

Say: "Knowledge of it is with my Lord alone, and none will reveal it when its time arrives but He. This is a weighty matter in the heavens and earth. It shall only come upon you suddenly."

(7:187) (Al-Wahidi)[15]

They said to the Messenger of God:

– Why does your Lord not reveal to you which low-priced items are about to go up in price, so that you can re-sell them at a profit? Why does he not indicate in advance the land that he desires to render barren, so that you can leave it for a land that he will make more fertile?

God revealed the reply:

Say: "I have no power to do myself good or harm save as God wills. Had I known the Unseen I would have done myself much good, and no harm would have touched me. I am merely a warner, and a herald of good tidings to a people who believe."

(7:188) (Al-Wahidi)[16]

Irritated, certain Meccans said:

– God is too great to choose as a Messenger a human such as Muhammad!

God revealed the reply:

We sent not before you save men to whom We revealed ...

(16:43) (Al-Zamakhshari)[17]

Ten

God orders combat against the polytheists

During the Meccan period, the Muslim community were subjected to increasing pressure from their clans. Nearly sixty of them had to seek exile in Abyssinia. The Prophet himself, after the death of his uncle, was isolated and weakened. Shortly afterwards his wife Khadija died. Without these two principal supporters, his life was in danger.

Rescue for the community came from the town of Yathrib, called Medina after the death of the Prophet.

There two main polytheistic tribes, Aws and Khazraj, had been engaged in a ruinous war since time immemorial. Their chiefs converted to Islam and called on Muhammad to arbitrate. They recognised his authority, inasmuch as it did not mean the victory of one of the two tribes over another, but rather that of a religion destined to transcend tribalism. They suggested that Muhammad leave his native town and settle in Yathrib.

The Prophet initially organised the "exodus" of his companions, and finally joined them at Yathrib with his faithful companion Abu Bakr. He became the head of a community whose message of monotheism was a challenge addressed to the principal polytheist tribes of Arabia. Tribal society was based on a logic whereby conflicts could be resolved only by war, unless a negotiated compromise could be found. As a compromise could not be found in the clash between Islam and polytheism, war swiftly followed.

From then on, God called on the believers, in cases of necessity and within certain limits, to bear arms and fight the infidels.

> **Fight in the cause of God those who fight you, but do not commit aggression: God loves not the aggressors. Slay them wherever you fall upon them, and expel them from where they had expelled you; apostasy by force is indeed more serious than slaying. Do not fight them near the Holy Mosque unless they fight you therein. If they fight you therein, slay them: such is the reward of unbelievers. But if they desist, then God is All-Forgiving, Compassionate to each. Fight them until there is no longer forced apostasy, and the religion is God's. If they desist, no aggression is permitted except against the wicked.**
>
> (Qur'an, 2:190–3)

The change of tone from one period to another is illustrated by the following episode:

> One day, when they were still at Mecca before the Hegira, several companions of the Prophet said to him:
> – Allow us therefore to defend ourselves against the infidels.
> The Prophet replied to them:
> – God orders me to pardon. Do not fight these people.
> After the Hegira, when God ordered the Prophet to fight the infidels, some of his companions retreated and took fright.

(Clan solidarity manifests itself here: the Muslims, called to combat the unbelievers, could not forget that they were also their brothers and their cousins. Hence their reticence to confront these unbelievers in a struggle to the death.)

Then God revealed this verse:

Have you not considered those to whom it was said: "Hold back from the fight, and perform prayer and pay the alms" and how, when fighting was decreed upon them, behold, a group among them were found to fear human beings as they fear God or even more? They say: "Our Lord, why have You decreed fighting upon us? If only You had deferred us for a short while." Say to them: "The delights of this life are brief, but the next

life is more excellent for those who are pious. Nor will you be wronged one fleck."

(4:77) (Al-Wahidi)[1]

Whoso fights in the cause of God and is killed, or else is victorious, We shall bestow upon him a magnificent wage.

(4:74)

Eight years after leaving Mecca, the Prophet came back as a victor. He granted temporary immunity to the tribes who still adhered to polytheism, even granting them the right to make the pilgrimage according to the pagan rite. The Prophet's thinking was that they should be given the necessary time to reflect, so that they would realise the failure of their idols and embrace Islam of their own accord.

However, a short time before the death of the Prophet, God himself put an end to this pact:

A proclamation from God and His Messenger to all mankind on the day of the Greater Pilgrimage:
God is quit of the polytheists, as is His Messenger. If you repent, this shall be better for you. If you turn away, know that you cannot evade the power of God. And announce to unbelievers a torment most painful. Except for those among the polytheists with whom you had a compact, and who never let you down, nor ever aided anyone against you – with them you are to fulfil

their compact until their appointed term. God loves the pious.

Once the sacred months are shorn, kill the polytheists wherever you find them, arrest them, imprison them, besiege them, and lie in wait for them at every site of ambush. If they repent, perform the prayer and pay the alms, let them go on their way: God is All-Forgiving, Compassionate to each.

(9:3–5)

Eleven

God replies to the arguments of the Jews

Settled in Yathrib, the Prophet and his Meccan companions were warmly welcomed by the members of the two
leading tribes of the city (Aws and Khazraj) who had converted to Islam. They were received less enthusiastically by
the members of these tribes, and some others who had not
converted or whose conversion was only superficial (the
Hypocrites).

The Prophet was confronted primarily by a politico-
religious challenge posed by the three Jewish tribes in
the city: Banu Quaynuqa, Banu al Nadir and the Banu
Quraydha. These tribes did not recognise him as the
Messenger of God and regarded him as a leader whose
growing power would challenge their long-standing status
and privileges.

Rich and well armed, they were however divided among themselves, and feared that by attacking the Prophet they would start a long war with the notables of Aws and Khazraj who had aligned themselves with the Prophet. They accepted the pact of understanding that the Prophet proposed to them, while harassing him with questions designed to lead him into doctrinal confusion.

However, in the answers that God inspired to the Prophet, He placed Islam in the continuing trajectory of Judaism and Christianity. He saw the three religions as expressions of His own Word. They are called religions of the Book, referring to the "original book" Umm al Kitab, that God has "in his presence" and from which all three religions are derived.

> Say: "We believe in God,
> And what has been revealed to us,
> And what has been revealed to Abraham, Ishmael, Isaac, Jacob and the Tribes;
> We believe in what was revealed to Moses and Jesus and the prophets from God.
> We do not distinguish between any of them.
> To Him we surrender."[1]
>
> (Qur'an, 3:84)

Salman the Persian had travelled for a long time in search of the God of Abraham. He had been in the service of several Christian priests of whom the last had announced the imminent arrival of a Prophet from an Arab tribe. Salman had in the end joined the Messenger of God in Yathrib, to embrace Islam in the Prophet's presence. Salman spoke to the Prophet about these priests, praising their qualities:

– Messenger of God, they continually fasted and prayed, they believed in you and announced your imminent coming as a prophet ...

When he had finished praising them, the Messenger of God said:

– Salman, they are destined for the flames of Hell.

It seemed to Salman that the earth became covered in darkness.

But the Almighty intervened, to say:

As for the believers, for the Jews, the Christians and the Sabeans[2] who believe in God and the Last Day, and who do righteous deeds – these have their wage with their Lord. No fear shall fall upon them, nor shall they grieve.

Hearing this verse, Salman said:

– It was as though the weight of a mountain had been lifted from my shoulders.

(2:62) (Al-'Asqalani)[3]

The Muslims were convinced that Jewish and Christian religious leaders had falsified previous Books (the Torah and the Gospel) that God had sent them, effacing in particular the passages announcing the coming of Muhammad. God made the following reproach to the

People of the Book:

O People of the Book, why do you blaspheme against the signs of God, though you witness them?
O People of the Book, why do you confound truth with falsehood, and conceal the truth, even though you know it?

(3:69–71)

The Prophet continued calling on the Jews to embrace Islam, warning them against the anger of God. They said to him:

– No, Muhammad, we shall follow rather the way of our ancestors. They were more knowledgeable than us and were superior to us.

Then God revealed these verses:

And when it is said to them: "Follow what God has brought down," they answer: "We would rather follow that which we found our ancestors have practised." How so, when their ancestors understood nothing, nor were rightly guided?

(2:170) (Ibn Ishaq)[4]

'Umar ibn al Khattab was one of the Prophet's companions, destined to become the second Caliph (successor) after the Prophet's death, and head of the Muslim community.

He possessed land on the heights of Yathrib. When he went there, he passed by Jewish schools. He went in and listened to what was being said. The Jews said to him:

– 'Umar, among the friends of Muhammad there is nobody that we love more than you. When you pass by our homes, you do us no harm.

'Umar answered:

– In God's name I do not come out of love for you or out of a desire to see you. I come to listen to you.

They questioned him and he questioned them. They asked him:

– What angel is the friend of your prophet?

'Umar answered:

– Gabriel.

– Among those who dwell in heaven, Gabriel is our enemy. It is he who reveals our secrets to Muhammad. When he comes to us, he brings war and famine. Our friend is Michael. When he comes to us, he brings peace and abundance.

– What does this mean? You recognise Gabriel as one of those who dwell in heaven and nevertheless you contest Muhammad?

'Umar went to see the Messenger of God who received him with these words:

– Son of al Khattab, do you want me to recite a verse that has just been revealed to me?

He recited:

Say: "Whoever is an enemy of Gabriel, let him know

that it was He Who made him descend upon your heart, by God's leave, confirming his revelation, a guidance and glad tidings to the faithful.

"Whoso is an enemy of God, His angels and messengers, of Gabriel and Michael, know that God is the enemy of unbelievers."

'Umar exclaimed:

– By my mother and father, by He who sends you with the truth, I was coming to inform you, but He in whom is all goodness and learning communicated it to you before me!

(2:97–8) (al-'Asqalani)[5]

With initially limited resources, the Muslim community in Yathrib was a rallying point for new, overwhelmingly poor, converts from different regions of Arabia. In order to meet their needs, the Prophet, who had no personal fortune, asked the richest notables, be they Muslims, polytheists and Jews, to lend him money. God encouraged him to do this, promising to reward those who were generous:

Who shall be the one who offers up to God a handsome loan, which God shall multiply for him many times over?

The Almighty having revealed this verse, a Jew from Yathrib exclaimed:

– The God of Muhammad is in need!

When 'Umar ibn al-Khattab learned of this insult, he

took his sword and went in search of the Jew who had pronounced those words.

God intervened to preach calm and indulgence:

Tell the believers to forgive those who do not fear the battle-days of God [the Last Judgement] ...

The Messenger of God immediately called 'Umar and said to him:

– Put down your sword, 'Umar.

Then he recited the verse that Gabriel had just revealed to him. 'Umar exclaimed:

– ... In the name of He who sends you with the Truth, my face will never again express anger.

(2:245, 45:14) (Al-Wahidi)[6]

A Jewish scholar came to see the Messenger of God and said to him:

– Muhammad, we know that God balances the heavens on a finger, the trees on a finger, the waters and the damp soil on a finger, all living creatures on a finger, and that he says: I am the sovereign power.

At these words, the Messenger of God laughed loudly. God had just revealed to him the following verses:

Nor have they esteemed God as He ought to be esteemed, when the whole earth shall be in His grasp the Day of Resurrection, and when the heavens shall be rolled up in His right hand. Glory be to Him, and may He be exalted far above what they associate with Him!

(39:67) (Al-Wahidi)[7]

Some Jews came to say to the Messenger of God:

– You say that you are a prophet, yet why do you not speak to God or look at him as Moses did? We shall believe in you only if you do that.

The Prophet answered:

– Moses did not look on Almighty God.

God had revealed to him:

It is not vouchsafed for any human being that God should address Him except through inspiration or from behind a veil, or else He sends a messenger who reveals what He wills, by His leave. He is Exalted, All-Wise.

(42:51) (Al-Zamakhshari)[8] (Al-Wahidi)[9]

Certain of the Jews came to see the Messenger of God and questioned him on the creation of the heavens and the earth. He said:

– God created the earth on Sunday and Monday, the mountains and their beneficial resources on Tuesday. On Wednesday he created the trees and the water. On Friday he created the stars, sun, and moon.

– And then, what happened?

– God sat on his throne.

– You would have been right had you added: Then He rested.

The Messenger of God became angry. [It is to offend God to claim that he needs to rest.]

Almighty God comforted him by revealing these verses:

We created the heavens and earth and what between in six days, and no weariness touched Us.

(50:38) (Al-Wahidi)[10]

Some Jews said to the Messenger of God:

– If you are a prophet, bring us a book that came down all at once from heaven, as Moses did.

This was the answer of Almighty God:

The People of the Book ask you to bring down upon them a book from heaven. But surely they asked Moses a thing even more outrageous than that. They said to him: "Show us God face to face," and were struck by lightning for their sin.

(4:153) (Muqatil[11] and Al-Zamakhshari)[12]

The Jews denigrated the Messenger of God, saying:

–This man's energy is given over to women and pleasure. Were he a prophet, as he claims, prophecy would have come before womanising!

Almighty God then revealed these verses:

We sent messengers before you to whom We gave spouses and progeny.

(13:38) (Al-Wahidi)[13]

The Jews of Yathrib finally joined the polytheistic enemies of the Prophet, and God addressed them in steadily more severe terms:

The Jews say, "The hand of God is shackled!" May their own hands be shackled and may they be cursed for what they say! Rather, His hands are spread forth and He dispenses in any manner He wishes.

(5:64)

We forbade them certain delectable foods which had been made licit to them; by reason, too, of their obstructing the path to God, repeatedly; their taking usury, though forbidden to do so; and their devouring the wealth of people dishonestly – to the unbelievers among them We have readied a painful torment.

(4:160–1)

Twelve

God replies to the arguments of the Christians

In Yathrib, the Muslims also engaged in vigorous debate with the Christians. The latter group lived in another city, Najran, and only rarely came to Yathrib. Christian debate with Muslims and Jews was doctrinal in character but without political or military implications. So it did not have the violent character of the debate between Muslims and Jews.

> Some Jews and Christians were together in the house of the Prophet. They began to engage in a polemical debate.
> The Jews said:
> – Abraham must have been Jewish.
> The Christians replied:
> – Abraham must have been Christian.
> The Almighty then revealed these verses to the Prophet:

O People of the Book, why do you dispute concerning Abraham? The Torah and evangel were revealed only after his time. Will you not be reasonable? Consider. It was you who argued about a matter of which you have knowledge. Why then do you argue about a matter of which you have no knowledge? God knows and you do not know. Abraham was neither a Jew nor a Christian, but a man of pristine faith, a Muslim, nor was he an idolator.

(Qur'an, 3:65–7) (Ibn Ishaq)[1]

On another day, in the house of the Messenger of God, one of the Jews said to the Christians:
– Your faith is baseless.
And he blasphemed against Jesus and the Gospel.
One of the Christians said to the Jews:
– It is your faith which is baseless.
He blasphemed against Moses and the Torah.
Then God revealed:
The Jews say the Christians count for nothing; the Christians say the Jews count for nothing; yet both recite the Book. The ignorant repeat their statements.
God shall judge between them on the Day of Resurrection regarding that upon which they differ.

(2:113) (Ibn Ishaq)[2]

A delegation of the sizeable Christian community in Najran came to Yathrib to meet the Messenger of God.

They arrived in the afternoon and immediately went to the Mosque where the Messenger of God had just finished praying. They were all clad in priests' vestments, in rich material from Yemen. The companions of the Prophet had never seen the like.

The time for prayer having arrived, they prepared to pray in the Mosque itself. The Muslims wanted to prevent them but the Messenger of God said:

– Let them pray.

After the prayer the Christians asked:

– Why do you insult our Lord Jesus?

– What do you mean?

– You say of him that he is a servant.

– Yes, he is the servant of God. His prophet ...

The Christians became angry. [They consider that Jesus is the Son of God.]

– Has anyone ever seen a human born without a father? If there is one, tell us his name ...

The Almighty dictated the reply of the Prophet:

The likeness of Jesus in God's sight is like Adam. He created him of dust then said to him "Be!" and he was.

(3:59) (Al-Wahidi)[3]

The Messenger of God said to the Christians:

– Embrace Islam.

They answered:

– We have already embraced Islam.

– No, you have not yet done this.

– We embraced Islam before you.

– You are lying. Three things separate you from Islam: you claim that God was born, you adore the cross, and you eat pork.

– Who is therefore the father of God, Muhammad?

The Messenger of God did not answer.

The next day he came to see them and recited what God had revealed to him in the meantime:

It is blasphemy they utter, those who say that God is Christ the son of Mary! For Christ had said: "O Children of Israel, worship God, my Lord and your Lord." Whoso ascribes partners to God, God proscribes the Garden to him, and his final refuge is the Fire. Wrongdoers shall have no champions.

It is blasphemy they utter, those who say that God is the third of three! There is no god except the One God.

(5:72) (Ibn Ishaq)[4]

Thirteen

God cares for the Muslim community

In Yathrib, the believers learned how to live according to the spirit of Islam. They encountered problems that they could no longer solve according to ancestral customs, but which they did not yet know how to solve, from a Muslim perspective. They therefore asked the Prophet for advice. They submitted all kinds of questions to him, even the most intimate.

He chose, according to each case, to answer the question himself or to await an answer from God. Sometimes the answer given by the Prophet was subsequently rectified by a divinely inspired verse.

In this way, the values and norms that structured the first Muslim community began to take shape.

On God's compassion for the believers:

If My worshippers ask you about Me, I am near.
I answer the prayer of him who prays when he prays to
Me.

(Qur'an, 2:186)

On the personal responsibility of each person in the eyes
of God:

Fear a Day in which you shall return to God, when each
soul shall be paid back that which it has earned. And
they shall not be wronged.

(2:281)

On the value of human life:

We decreed to the Children of Israel that he who kills
a soul neither in revenge for another, nor to prevent
corruption on earth, it is as if he killed the whole of
mankind; whereas he who saves a soul, it is as if he has
saved the whole of mankind.

(5:32)

A young Abyssinian slave was going to the Mosque to
pray. The Messenger of God noticed his assiduous attend-
ance and was surprised one day not to see him there. He
asked the slave's master:
  – Where is the boy?
  – He has fever, Messenger of God.

– Well then, let us visit him!

The Messenger of God and several of his companions went immediately to visit the boy. Some days later, the Messenger of God noticed that the slave had not returned and he asked his master:

– How is the boy?

– He is in the same state.

The Messenger of God went to visit the boy again, who died in his arms. The Messenger washed his body for burial, wrapped him in a shroud and buried him. Many companions were surprised. The Muhājirūn[1] said:

– We have left our houses, our property and our parents. We have not seen anyone of our number receive a similar treatment to that which this boy received.

The Ansār[2] said:

– We gave hospitality to the Prophet, we protected him and supported him. And now he gives preference to an Abyssinian slave.

The Almighty revealed:

The noblest among you in God's sight are the most pious.

(49:13) (Al-Wahidi)[3] (Al-Zamakhshari)[4]

A Muslim woman came to see the Prophet and said to him:

– Messenger of God, the women are distressed.

– Why?

– Because the Qu'ran does not speak highly of them as it does in the case of men.

Then God revealed:

Muslim men and Muslim women,
Believing men and believing women,
Devout men and devout women,
Sincere men and sincere women,
Patient men and patient women,
Humble men and humble women,
Charitable men and charitable women,
Fasting men and fasting women,
Men who guard their chastity, and women who guard their chastity,
Men who often remember God, and women who often remember God,
To all of them God has made ready a pardon and a glorious reward.

(33:35) (Al-Wahidi[5]; variant: Muqatil)[6]

This is a verse of fundamental importance. From a spiritual point of view, men and women in Islam are equal in the eyes of God.

Before the rules to be followed during the Ramadan fast were laid down, Muslims could eat, drink, and have sexual relations with their wives until the moment they fell asleep. After this they had to abstain until the breaking of the fast the following evening. One evening, 'Umar, a close companion of the Prophet, infringed this rule: waking up during the night, he could not help having sexual relations with his wife.

The next day he went to see the Prophet and said to him:

– I have come to implore God and his Prophet ...

– What have you done wrong?

– I could not help having sexual relations with my wife last night ... can you show me a path to pardon?

The Prophet said simply:

– I did not expect this from you, 'Umar ...

'Umar went back home.

Shortly afterwards, the Prophet knew that 'Umar was not the only person to infringe the rule of abstinence. Several Muslims confessed that they had done the same as 'Umar. The Prophet recalled 'Umar and recited the following verse:

It is licit to you, on a night of fasting, to lie down with your wives. They are as a garment to you, and you are as a garment to them. God knows you used to cheat, but He has turned His face towards you and forgiven you. But now go in and lie with them, and seek what God has foreordained for you, and eat and drink until the white streak of dawn can be distinguished from the black streak. Then complete your fast until night-time. Do not lie with them in periods when you retire for devotional prayers in mosques.

These are the bounds set by God: do not infringe them.

(2:187) (Muqatil)[7]

God does not only treat sinners indulgently and forgive their wrongdoing but He even changes the existing moral rules, permitting what had hitherto been forbidden.

'A'isha, the daughter of Abu Bakr, the closest companion of the Prophet, was the Prophet's favourite wife.

This is her story:

During an expedition the Messenger of God ordered a halt in a waterless place. There I lost one of my necklaces. I told the Prophet of this. He decided to prolong the halt until the following day. This provoked anger on the part of some people, who said:

– It is 'A'isha's fault.

They went to see my father, Abu Bakr:

– Do you see what 'A'isha has done? She is delaying us and the Messenger of God in an arid place at a time when we have no water and cannot make our ablutions ...

Abu Bakr came to me and repeated these words going so far as to slap me on the stomach, while I had to remain immobile, the Messenger of God having fallen asleep with his head on my thigh.

Then God revealed the verse authorising ablutions without water:

[If] you do not find water, then use some clean earth and wipe your faces and hands.

Then the Messenger of God said:

– Before us, people prayed in their houses or in their

sanctuaries. For us the whole earth becomes suitable for purification, wherever we may be when the hours of prayer arrives.

(4:43) (Al-Wahidi)[8]

God intervenes at a given moment, so as believers can resolve a sudden problem. Muslims thus had the impression that God was listening to them in their daily lives.

During the period of Jāhiliyya [the pre-Islamic "period of ignorance"] and in early Islam, a person coming back from the pilgrimage and still in a state of ritual consecration, did not enter a house, a tent, or a garden by the front door, but had to go through an entrance put in place at the back. Only the members of certain tribes were exempt from this obligation.

They were called "ahmusi'" Exercising his right to this exemption, the Prophet entered a house by the front door. He was immediately followed by a man in a state of ritual consecration, whose arrival provoked general disapproval. He said to the Messenger of God:

– I have only imitated what you did.

– But I am an "ahmusi"

– I too am an "ahmusi".

Subsequently God revealed these verses:

It is not a virtue that you approach houses from their backs. Virtue is to be pious. So approach houses from the front, and fear God – perhaps you will achieve your quest.

(2:189) (Al-Wahidi)[9]

This divine intervention was in response to a question closely linked to the Arab context of the time.

> During one of his sermons, the Messenger of God evoked the Last Judgement in terms so terrible that people left in tears, terrified. Ten of the closest companions of the Prophet, among them Abu Bakr, 'Ali ibn Abu Talib, Abu Dhar al-Ghifari and Salman the Persian, met and swore before God that henceforth they would fast during the day and pray at night; they would no longer sleep on couches, eat meat or fat, or have sexual relations with their wives. They would wear homespun robes, renounce the pleasures of this world and live scattered across the world, living as solitary monks, devoted to the adoration of God. When the Messenger of God heard this he called them together and said:
>
> – Is it true that you have made all these decisions?
>
> – We wish to dedicate our lives to doing good.
>
> – These matters have not been the object of divine commands! You have rights towards your families! Fast but eat as well! Pray and sleep! I pray and sleep, I fast and eat, even meat and fat. He who leaves my path is no longer one of my followers.
>
> In his following sermon he said:
>
> – What should one think of those who forsake the company of women, who give up foods and tasty dishes, sleep and all life's pleasures? I do not order you to become priests or monks. My religion does not forbid women or

meat or oblige you to live in hermits' cells ... piety consists of striving in the service of God. Adore Him and associate no one with Him, accomplish the Pilgrimage, great or small, pray, give alms, fast during the month of Ramadan. Those who were rigorous with themselves have consumed their strength, as God was rigorous towards them. You will find their remnant in monasteries and hermitages.

The Almighty revealed:

– O believers, forbid not such good things as God has permitted you ...

They said:

– We have sworn an oath. How can we now desist?

The Almighty revealed:

God will not take you to task for a muddle in your oaths ...

(5:87, 89) (Muqatil)[10] (Al-Wahidi)[11]

An example of divine intervention in a conversation between the Prophet and his companions.

One of the Ansars said to the Messenger of God:

– How is it that the crescent of the moon appears initially as thin as a thread, then grows to form a perfect circle, then shrinks to its original size? Why does it not retain the same form?

God then revealed these verses:

They ask you about the new moons.

Say: "They are times appointed for mankind, and the Pilgrimage."

(2:189) (Al-Wahidi)[12]

A man went to see 'Umar ibn al-Khattab and said to him:

– A woman came to ask me to sell her some dates for a dirham. She was pleasing to me. I answered:

– In my house I have better dates than these. Come in.

I took her into my house, aware that her husband was away on God's service. I obtained all that I wanted from her, except complete possession of her body.

'Umar said:

– Woe on you. Her husband is away on the service of God?

– Yes.

– Go and see Abu Bakr.

The man went to see Abu Bakr and repeated to him what he had said to 'Umar.

Abu Bakr said:

– Go and seek the Messenger of God.

The man went and recounted his story to the Messenger of God, who asked him:

– Her husband is away on the service of God?

– Yes.

The Messenger of God withdrew without saying anything.

Then God revealed these verses:

Perform the prayer at the two ends of the day and for some hours of the night.

Good deeds efface bad deeds.

When the verse was recited to him the man asked the Messenger of God:

– Is this verse addressed to me or does it concern everyone?

'Umar patted him on the chest and said:

– No, this verse does not apply only to you, it concerns everyone.

The Messenger of God burst out laughing and said:

– 'Umar has spoken the truth.

(11:114) (Al-Wahidi)[13]

Yathrib went through a period of penury: prices went up and the people were hungry.

Duhayya al Kalbi returned from Syria at the head of a caravan and ordered that drums be beaten in the street to warn people of his arrival. It was Friday midday and the Messenger of God was preaching in the Mosque. People rose up and went running out to join the caravan which was coming into the city. There were only twelve men in the Mosque among whom were Abu Bakr and 'Umar.

The Almighty revealed these verses:

When they spot some commerce or frivolity, they rush towards it and leave you standing.

Say: "What is with God is better than frivolity or commerce, and God is the best of providers."

(62:11) (Al-Zamakhshari)[14] (Al-Wahidi)[15]

A man came to see the Prophet and said:

– What can we do with a dinar?

The Prophet answered:

– Spend it on yourself.

– What can I do with a second dinar?

– Spend it on your family

– What should I do with a third dinar?

– Spend it on the person who serves you.

–With a fourth dinar?

– Spend it on your father and mother.

– With a fifth dinar?

– Spend it on your relatives

– A sixth dinar?

– Spend it in the service of God: this is the best course of action.

Then the Almighty revealed these verses:

They ask you what they should spend. Say: "What you spend of wealth goes to parents, near kin, orphans, the poor and the needy wayfarer." God is well aware of any good you do.

(2:215) (Al-Wahidi)[16]

The houses of Yathrib being too small, people had to go outside to answer the call of nature. Women went out at nightfall. Dissolute individuals followed them, approached them and made advances to them. When the women remained silent these men became even more importunate. When the women repelled their advances, they finally gave up and went away.

These scoundrels pursued in particular slaves, but in the darkness they could not distinguish free women from slaves since they all wore robes and head-coverings.

The women told their husbands of this and they in turn spoke to the Prophet.

The Almighty revealed these verses:

O Prophet, tell your wives, your daughters and women believers to wrap their outer garments closely around them, for this makes it more likely that they will be recognised and not be harassed.

(33:59) (Al-Wahidi)[17]

It is a question here of outer garments (*jilbab*) rather than a veil or a screen (*hijab*), a word that shall appear elsewhere in the Qur'an (33:53), applying only to the wives of the Prophet.

Before the Hegira, when a male inhabitant of Yathrib died and left a widow, the custom was that one of his sons by another wife or one of the deceased man's relations, covered the woman with his garment and married her. He enjoyed thereafter more rights over her than she herself or any other person. If he so decided he could marry her, without giving her a dowry other than that left by her late husband, or take this from her and give her nothing, or ignore and even mistreat her so that she would buy back her freedom by paying him the dowry as a ransom. He could also wait until she died so that he would inherit her property.

Abu Qays ibn al Aslat died after the Hegira. His widow

was called Kubaysha. One of the sons of her late husband by another woman covered her with his garment and married her. Then he ceased having sexual relations with her and looking after her, hoping that she would, in the end, buy back her freedom from him.

Kubaysha went to see the Messenger of God and said to him:

– My husband is dead and his son inherited me as wife. Much time has passed and he does not want to look after me or have sexual relations with me, or give me my freedom.

The Messenger of God answered:

– Go home until the commandment of God concerning you is revealed.

She went home, while other women, learning of her plight, went and said to the Messenger of God:

– We are in the same plight as Kubaysha at the hands of the sons of our late husbands or of his cousins.

The Almighty revealed these verses:

O believers, it is not licit for you to inherit women against their will, nor must you coerce them so as to take possession of part of what you had given them, unless they commit manifest adultery. Live with them in kindness. And if you come to loathe them, perhaps you may loathe something in which God places abundant good ... Do not marry women that your fathers had married ...

(4:19, 22) (Al-Wahidi)[18]

As a more humane approach to the position of women, we may note this phrase, often repeated by the Prophet: "Go home until the commandment of God concerning you has been revealed."

The intervention of God in human affairs is perceived as self-evident.

> The Prophet went to visit a sick Muslim, who said to him:
> – To whom shall I bequeath my property, I who have neither father nor son?
> On this occasion God revealed:
> **They will ask thee for a pronouncement. Say: "God pronounces to you concerning the indirect heirs. If a man perishes having no children, but he has a sister, she shall receive a half of what he leaves, and he is her heir if she has no children. If there be two sisters, they shall receive two-thirds of what he leaves; if there be brothers and sisters, the male shall receive the portion of two females ..."**
>
> (4:176) (Muqatil)[19]

On polygamy:

> **Marry whoever pleases you among women – two, three or four; but if you fear you will not be fair to them all, then one only, or else what you own of slaves. This would be closer to impartiality.**
>
> (4:3)

The wife of Sa'd ibn al Rabi' was disrespectful towards her husband, who struck her. She complained to her father. He brought her to the Messenger of God and said to him:

– My daughter was disrespectful towards her husband. He struck her.

The Messenger of God said:

– Let her do the same to him!

The father and daughter went away, but shortly afterwards the Messenger of God called them back and said:

– Gabriel has just visited me. God reveals these verses:

Men are legally responsible for women, inasmuch as God has preferred some over others in bounty, and because of what they spend from their wealth. Thus, virtuous women are obedient, and preserve their trusts, such as God wishes them to be preserved. And those you fear may rebel, admonish, and abandon them in their beds, and smack them. If they obey you, seek no other way against them.

(4:34) (Al-Wahidi)[20] (Al-Zamakhshari)[21]

We have noted earlier that the Qur'an recognises the equality of men and women in terms of metaphysics and eschatology. They possess an equal spiritual dignity. In the above case it confirms their social inequality. This is an example of a compromise solution between God's law and the prevailing tribal and patriarchal customs of the time. It is a striking example of the way that divine transcendence is inscribed in human temporality.

Another example is the way that slavery survived while the Qur'an encouraged the release of slaves:

> **No believer is to kill another save in error. Whoever kills a believer in error, the freeing of a believing slave is decreed and blood-money handed over to his kin, unless the latter forgo this as an act of charity. If he belongs to a clan which is your enemy while he is a believer, the freeing of a believing slave is decreed.**
>
> (4:92)

Fourteen

God guides His Messenger

While he was still in Mecca, the Prophet was talking one day with al-Walid ibn al Mughira, one of the lords of Quraysh [the principal Meccan tribe]. A man called Ibn Umm Maktum, who was blind, approached them and said to the Prophet, "Messenger of God, teach me what God taught you." Receiving no response, and unable to see to whom Muhammad was talking, he repeated his question several times, pulling the sleeve of the Prophet. The latter finally became annoyed. He frowned and moved away from the blind man and continued to speak to al-Walid.

The Prophet received this reproach from God:

He frowned and turned aside
When the blind man approached him.
But how do you know? Perhaps he was seeking to

cleanse his sins,
Or else be admonished, and the Remembrance might
profit him.

As for him whose wealth has made him vain,
To him you turn your full attention.
And yet it is not up to you if he does not cleanse his
sins.
But he who came to you in earnest endeavour, in piety,
From him you are distracted.

No indeed! This is a Reminder –
Whoso desire may remember it ...

Subsequently the Prophet was very kind towards Ibn
Umm Maktum, addressing these words to him:
– Greetings to him who brought down on me the criti-
cism of my Lord.
(Qur'an, 80:1–12) (Al-Wahidi)[1] (Al-Zamakhshari)[2]

God intervenes to "blame" his Prophet, reminding him
that a pious man has precedence over a powerful man:

Among the first Muslims were some individuals who did
not belong to a clan [slaves or freedmen]. The notables of
Mecca said:
– Look at these people who follow Muhammad! They
are just freed slaves or slaves, the sweepings of the areas
in which we live. We would follow Muhammad if he

addressed the chiefs of these areas and the former owners of the freed slaves. Then they said to Abu Talib, uncle of the Prophet:

– Tell your nephew to chase away these strangers and tramps if he wants to gain the attention of the chiefs and lords of his people.

Abū Tālib passed the message on to his nephew:

– If only you distanced yourself from these people.'

Then God intervened:

And do not drive away those who call upon their Lord morning and evening, seeking His face ... If you drive them away you would be unjust.

(6:52) (Muqatil)[3]

According to Al-Zamakhshari, on the advice of 'Umar, one of his closest companions, the Prophet initially agreed to debar freed slaves.

The polytheists demanded:

– Confirm this for us in writing!

The Prophet reportedly asked 'Ali to bring a parchment scroll in order to set this decision [to exclude freed slaves] in writing. At this point, the Qur'anic verse **"Do not reject those who pray"** was revealed. The Prophet immediately tore up the parchment and 'Umar excused himself.

(Al-Zamakhshari)[4]

Shortly before the Hegira, the Messenger of God had a dream in which he left for an abundantly irrigated land covered in palm trees and fruit trees. He recounted his dream to his companions who rejoiced at the prospect. They waited for some time and, as nothing happened, said:

– Messenger of God, when do we leave for the country that you saw in a dream?

He did not answer.

Then God revealed:

Say: "I am a novelty among messengers. I know not what is to be done to me or you. I merely follow what is revealed to me."

(46:9) (Al-Wahidi)[5]

Thus, God intervenes in the way the Prophet takes decisions.

Once in Yathrib, the Muslims continued to pray as they did in Mecca, turning towards Jerusalem. The Messenger of God said one day to Gabriel:

– I would like the Almighty to free me of the obligation to turn towards the qibla [direction of prayer] of the Jews and give me another.

The Messenger was thinking about the Kaaba which had been the qibla of Abraham. Gabriel said to him:

– I, like you, am only a servant of God. I have no power. Ask your Lord to designate Abraham's qibla as the direction of prayer.

Gabriel rose up into the heavens and the Prophet kept his eyes turned towards the sky in the hope that the Angel would come and inform him that his prayer had been answered. For the past sixteen months the Muslims, having emigrated from Mecca to Yathrib, had turned towards Jerusalem while praying. Then the Almighty revealed to his Messenger these verses:

We have seen you turning your face from side to side in the heavens,

So We will now turn you towards a direction that will please you:

Turn your face towards the Sacred Mosque.

Wherever you may be, turn your faces towards it.

When this verse was revealed the Messenger of God was in the Mosque of the Banu Salma. He had just completed two prostrations of the midday prayer. He changed immediately the direction of the prayer and men took the place hitherto reserved for women, while women took that reserved for men. From that moment on the mosque was called the Mosque of two qiblas.

(2:144) (Al-Zamakhshari)[6]

Some Jews came to see the Messenger of God and said to him:

– Muhammad, tell us what turned you away from the qibla towards which you formerly turned when praying, you who claim to follow the religion of Abraham? Should you return to the qibla that you have just abandoned we shall follow you and we shall believe you.

Then God revealed:

Foolish people shall say: "What turned them away from the direction of prayer they once followed?"

Say: "To God belongs the East and the West. He guides whosoever He will onto a straight path."

(2:142) (Ibn Ishaq)[7]

At Yathrib the Messenger was embarrassed by material demands that he was unable to meet. Seeing this, the Ansar said to one another:

– The man whom the Almighty has sent to us and who is our nephew has expenses that he cannot meet. Let us give some of our surplus to him.

They set apart some of their property and set to see the Messenger of God. They said to him:

– You are our nephew. God sent you to us to lead us on the path of righteousness. You are in difficulty, with expenses that you cannot meet. We have thought fit to set apart some of our property and offer it to you so that you may use as you see fit. Here it is.

At this point God revealed:

Say: "I ask you no wage for it save amity of kinship."

(42:23) (Al-Wahidi)[8]

After the battle of Uhud [the only major battle lost by the Prophet] the Messenger of God saw that the body of his uncle Hamza had been terribly mutilated. This was the greatest distress he had experienced. Standing over the body of his uncle he said:

– May God have pity on you. You have honourably observed the bonds of kinship and you always did good for others. Were it not for the sadness of your family I would have preferred to leave you where you lie, that traces of your body be found in countless other bodies. Almighty God, if you give me victory over these people, I shall inflict on seventy of them the suffering that they inflicted on Hamza.

Then the Almighty revealed:

And if you punish, you are to punish with the like of what you were punished.

(16:126) (Al-Wahidi)[9] (Muqatil)[10]

Safiyya bint Akhtab, one of the Prophet's Jewish wives, came and said to him:

– Messenger of God, your wives are harassing me, saying "Jewess! Daughter of a Jewess!"

The Prophet answered:

– Tell them: "My father is Aaron, Moses is my uncle, and Muhammad my husband."

The Almighty revealed these verses:

O believers, let no group make fun of another, for they may be better than them.

Let no women make fun of other women, for they may be better than them.

Refrain from backbiting one another, and from calling each other by nicknames.

(49:11) (Al-Zamakhshari)[11]

A boy came to see the Messenger of God and said to him:

– My mother asks you for some clothes.

The Messenger of God answered:

– At this time we have nothing, not even a shirt. At any time God may send us something. Come back later.

The boy conveyed this reply to his mother who said in her turn:

– Tell him: my mother asks you to give me the shirt that you are wearing.

When the Prophet heard this, he went home, took off his shirt, and offered it to the boy.

Then the Almighty revealed these verses:

Let not your hand be chained to your neck, nor spread it out as far as it extends, or else you will end up worthy of blame, regretful.

(17:29) (Al-Zamakhshari)[12]

The Prophet recited to the Muslims the Qur'an that had been revealed to him. His companions were henceforth forbidden to evoke the exploits of the warriors of the past, or to speak highly of the tribal conflicts which had opposed the Arabs among themselves in the past. They said to him one day:

Messenger of God, could you tell us some stories?

The Almighty revealed:

We narrate to you the fairest of narratives, through what We revealed to you – this Qur'an.

And yet before it you were heedless.

(12:3) (Al-Wahidi)[13]

The Thaqif sent a delegation to the Prophet whose task was to negotiate the conditions of their entry into the Muslim community. They said to him:

– We shall only accept your authority if you grant us privileges which maintain our prestige among the Arabs. We shall continue to receive the interest on the loans we granted while being relieved of our own debts. We shall worship our goddess Al-Lat for a year and we shall not be required to destroy her statue at the end of this period. During this time we shall be exempted from taking part in your military campaigns and paying legally required alms ... when the Arabs ask you why you accorded us such privileges you will answer: it is God who ordered me.

They produced a piece of parchment which they gave to the scribe. The Prophet began to dictate:

– In the name of God, the Clement and Merciful, this is a text of Muhammad, the Messenger of God, addressed to the Thaqif ... they will not be compelled to fight.

They insisted:

– Nor to pay the legally required alms ...

The Prophet fell silent.

They said to the scribe:

– Write: nor to pay the alms required by law ...

The scribe looked at the Prophet.

Irritated, 'Umar broke the silence and pulling his sword

from his scabbard, said:

– People of Thaqif, you are causing the Prophet distress. May God bring down suffering on your hearts.

They replied:

– We are not addressing you, but the Prophet.

Then the Almighty revealed:

There was a time when they almost beguiled you away from what We had revealed to you, to falsely ascribe to Us something different, whereupon they would have taken you for a friend. Had We not made you stand firm, you were about to lean a little towards them. Had you done so, We would have made you taste a double torment in this world, and double after death, and then you would have found no one to help you against Us.

(17:73–5) (Al-Zamakhshari)[14]

God intervenes in the course of events as they unfold, preventing the Prophet from giving in to the pressure of the Thaqif. He then reproaches the Prophet, threatening him with a punishment if he had ceded to them.

The Messenger of God had Mariyya brought to him and made love to her in the apartments of his wife Hafsa, in her absence. She came back early enough to surprise them. She told the Prophet of her sadness. Embarrassed, he murmured:

– Say nothing about this to 'A'isha. I shall refrain from having sexual relations with this woman.

Hafsa however quickly told 'A'isha, who immediately

went and told the other wives of the Prophet. The Messenger of God learned this, became angry, and announced that he would refrain from relations with all his wives for a month. God revealed these verses:

O Prophet, why forbiddest thou what God has made lawful to thee?

Then He revealed:

And when the Prophet confided to one of his wives a certain matter; and then, when she told of it, and God disclosed that to him, he made known part of it, and turned aside from part; then, when he told her of it, she said, "Who told thee this?" He said, "I was told of it by the All-knowing, the All-aware."

(66:1, 3) (Al-Wahidi)[16] (Al-Zamakhshari)[17]

God participates directly in the events of the Prophet's life; initially, He informs the Prophet of what happened without his knowledge, then tells the believers the conclusion of the incident.

A companion recounts the following incident:
The Prophet passed one door in front of our house and saw that we were laughing uproariously. He addressed these words of reproach to us:

– What is causing you to laugh so much?

Then he continued on his way. He soon came back and said to us:

– Gabriel, may the peace of God be upon him, came to say to me: O Muhammad the Almighty asks you: why do you drive to despair those who adore me?

Proclaim to my servants: "It is I Who am All-Forgiving, Compassionate to Each; that My torment is the most painful."

(15:49) (Al-Wahidi)[18]

'Abd Allah ibn Ubayy was one of the hypocrites, embracing Islam without believing in it. He was, however, one of the notables of the tribe of Khazraj, and this was the reason why the Prophet consistently sought to cultivate good relations with him.

When he died the Prophet came to his tomb and prepared to pronounce a blessing over it. 'Umar stood before him and said:

– Messenger of God, did the Almighty not forbid you to pray for the hypocrites? Are you going to bless this enemy of God, who has betrayed you so many times?

The Messenger of God merely smiled.

'Umar insisted and he finally said to him:

– Do not insist, 'Umar. God gave me the choice and I chose. He said to me: **"Whether you ask forgiveness for them or whether you do not, were you to ask forgiveness for them seventy times, God would not forgive them."**

The Messenger of God added:

– Had I known that if I asked more than seventy times God would pardon him, I would have done so.

He blessed 'Abd Allah ibn Ubayy, attended his burial,

and prayed before his tomb. 'Umar was surprised at the Prophet's boldness and said to himself:

– God and His Messenger are more knowledgeable than I am.

However, a little later God revealed:

You are never to pray over any one of them who dies, nor stand over his grave, for they disbelieved in God and His Messenger, and died as sinners.

Thereafter the Messenger of God did not bless a single hypocrite nor pray at his tomb.

(9:80, 84) (Al-Wahidi)[19]

The Muslims had gathered in the plain of al-Hudaybiyya and the time for midday prayer had come. Their enemies were led by Khalid ibn al Walid who had placed the horsemen of Quraysh so that they were opposite the Muslims when they turned towards Mecca. Bilal gave the call to prayer, the Messenger of God turned towards Mecca and the Muslims aligned themselves behind him, kneeling and prostrating themselves after him. At the conclusion of the time of prayer they dispersed and returned to their positions.

Khalid ibn al Walid remarked:

– They were no longer on their guard. Had we launched a charge against them, we could have inflicted heavy losses. Prayer is more sacred for them than their lives or the lives of their children.

Before the next time of prayer, that of the afternoon,

Gabriel communicated this verse to the Prophet:

If you happen to be present among them, and stand to lead them in prayer, let a group among them stand with you, and let them take up their arms. When they prostrate themselves in prayer let them be in the rear and let another group who have not yet prayed come forward to pray with you; let them be on their guard and take up their weapons. The unbelievers long for you to be negligent with your weapons and equipment, and thus would attack you in one rush.

The Prophet conducted the next prayer according to what had been revealed to him.

(4:102) (Al-Wahidi)[20]

The Messenger of God said:

– The things of this world have been revealed to me. I see how events unfold among my people until Judgement Day. The links of kinship among all the Arabs have been revealed to me. I know the ancestors of each one of you.

A man rose and asked:

– What is my destiny?

– Paradise.

Another man asked:

– And I?

– Paradise.

A third man asked:

– And I?

– You are destined for hell.

The man left the mosque, plunged into despair.

'Abd Allāh, son of Khuzayma, whose paternity was questioned by some people, rose to his feet and asked:

– Who is my father?

– Your father is indeed Khuzayma.

A son of 'Abd al Dar asked:

– And I, who is my father?

– Your father is Sa'd.

He had thus just learned that his real father was not the person he had thought.

'Umar ibn al Khattab then rose to his feet and addressed the Prophet:

– Messenger of God, it is better to protect us from certain truths ... we are only just emerging from ignorance and idolatry...

The Prophet nodded:

– Well spoken.

The Almighty revealed:

O believers, ask not about matters which, if revealed to you, would displease you.

(5:101) (Muqatil)[21]

Zayd ibn Haritha was adopted by the Messenger of God, having been a freed slave formerly belonging to the Prophet. He asked him:

– Prophet of God, marry me.

The Messenger of God asked him:

– Is there a woman who pleases you?

– Zaynab bint Jahsh.

– You are right. In her beauty and nobility converge. I shall ask for her to be your wife.

Zaynab, who was one of the Prophet's cousins, protested:

– I, the most accomplished woman of Quraysh, do not wish to marry a freed slave.

Her brother, who had to give his consent, was equally unwilling. The Messenger of God gave his definitive judgement:

– I have approved Zayd as a husband for Zaynab. It is my decision that you will marry him.

God revealed these verses:

It is not for any believer, man or woman, if God and His Prophet decide some matter, to have liberty of choice in action. Whoso disobeys God and His Prophet has strayed far in manifest error.

Zayd married Zaynab and had sexual relations with her. He complained afterwards of her coldness towards him. The Prophet decided to go to her home, to reason with her. When he saw her, he found her beautiful and attractive. God had decided that this should be so. When Zayd returned to complain again about her, the Prophet said:

– Keep your spouse and venerate God.

His heart murmured something else to him. One day he went to knock at the door of Zayd's house. Zaynab appeared in the entrance wearing only a robe, in order to tell him that Zayd was absent. He went home filled with desire, saying:

– Praise be to Almighty God who disposes of our hearts!

When Zayd learned from his wife what had happened,

he went to see the Prophet and said:

– Allow me to separate from my wife

The Prophet repeated:

– Keep your spouse and venerate God.

Zayd left, but broke off all contact with his wife.

God then revealed these verses:

Remember when you said to him to whom God had been generous, and you had been generous: "Retain your wife, and be pious before God" – all the while hiding within yourself what God was to reveal, and fearing people, though God is more worthy of your fear.

Thus, when Zayd had satisfied his desire for her, We gave her in marriage to you ...

(33: 36, 37) (Muqatil)[22]

This was a divine intervention, in "real time", in the earthly lives of the Prophet, of Zaynab, of Zayd. And Zaynab underlined proudly the privilege that was hers as a result of this intervention.

After her marriage to the Prophet, Zaynab said:

– None other of the Prophet's wives can be compared to me. They have all been married with dowries, under parental authority. I was married by a decree of God and his Prophet. God has revealed this in His Book, which is recited by all Muslims and which cannot be changed ...

(Ibn Sa'd)[23]

Fifteen

Verses concerning the person of the Prophet

A certain number of verses exist which concern the person of the Prophet and the respect due to him during his life on earth. It is difficult to see how believers today can literally adopt the prescriptions these verses contain.

At Yathrib, a delegation of the Banu Tamim tribe wanted to see the Prophet at midday while he was in bed. They called in a loud voice: "Muhammad, come out!"

The Messenger of God went out to see them. But the Almighty revealed:

They who call out to you from behind the chambers – most have no understanding. If only they had been patient until you came out to them, it would have been better for them.

(Qur'an, 49:4–5) (Al-Wahidi)[1] (Al-Zamakhshari)[2]

'Umar and Abu Bakr had a quarrel and their voices were raised in the presence of the Messenger of God. Following this the Almighty revealed:

O believers, raise not your voices above the voice of the Prophet, and do not speak loudly to him, as you speak loudly to one another, lest your works founder, and you are unaware of it.

(49:2) (Al-Wahidi)[3]

The Prophet heard Talha ibn 'Ubayd Allah, one of his companions, say:

– By God, if Muhammad dies and I am still alive, I shall marry 'A'isha.

God revealed:

You must not offend the Prophet, nor must you ever marry his wives after him, for such would be a mighty sin in the sight of God.

(33:53) (Al-Wahidi)[4] (Al-Zamakhshari)[5]

The believers are those who believe in God and His Messenger. If they are with him on some common endeavour, they should not depart until they ask his permission. Those who ask your permission are the ones who believe in God and His Messenger. If they ask your permission to attend to some affair of theirs, grant permission to whomever of them you wish, and ask God's forgiveness for them.

(24:62)

O Prophet, We have made licit for you the wives to whom you have given their bridal money, as also the slaves that God assigned you as war booty, the daughters of your paternal uncles and aunts, the daughters of your maternal uncles and aunts, who emigrated with you, and also a believing woman if she offers herself to the Prophet, provided the Prophet wishes to marry her, as a special dispensation to you only, but not to the believers ... You may defer any of them if you wish, and take in any of them you wish. And should you desire any of those you had deferred, no blame attaches to you ... Henceforth it is not licit for you to take more wives, nor to exchange them for other wives even if you admire their beauty – except for slaves. God watches closely over all things.

(33:50–3)

At the marriage of the Prophet with Zaynab bint Jahsh, there was a feast at which bread and meat were served. People arrived, ate, and left, leaving their places for those who came afterwards. During this time the new wife of the Prophet had her face turned to the wall. At the end [of the feast] three men remained in the house, engaged in an interminable conversation. Their presence became a source of irritation. The Prophet said nothing and went out. Only then did the men realise that their presence was a source of unease. Then the Prophet went to the apartments of Zaynab. Anas ibn Malik, his freedman, wanted to follow him. The Prophet however let a curtain fall behind him.

And God revealed:

O believers, enter not the chambers of the Prophet for a meal unless given leave, and do not wait around for it to be well cooked. Rather, if invited enter, and when fed disperse, not lingering for conversation. This behaviour irritates the Prophet, who is embarrassed to tell you, but God is not embarrassed by the truth. And if you ask his wives for some favour, do so from behind a screen; this is more chaste for both your hearts and theirs.

(33:53) (Al-Zamakhshari)[6]

Sixteen

Verses concerning the contemporaries of the Prophet

We observed in the preceding chapter that certain verses related to the person of the Prophet are no longer of relevance today. This is even truer of verses concerning the Prophet's contemporaries, mentioned by name in the Qur'an. Insofar as these verses refer to ordinary human beings, situated in the history of the seventh century, they cannot be followed "to the letter".

Very early in his preaching, the Prophet spoke severely to a crowd of Meccans:

– I must warn you of the imminence of a terrible punishment ... I can be of no benefit to you in this world, or of help in the next, if you do not say: "There is no God but God!"

This declaration provoked the wrath of his uncle, Abu Lahab, who cursed the Prophet.

– May you die before the day is out! Is it for this reason that you have gathered us together?

God came to the help of the Prophet, in response to this curse:

Perish the hands of Abu Lahab[1] – and perish he!
His wealth shall not avail him,
Not what he earned.
He shall be scorched by a fire, ablaze,
As too his wife, carrying the faggots;
Around her neck is a rope of fire.

(Qur'an, 111:1–5) (Ibn Kathir)[2]

God condemns an enemy of the Prophet, and his wife, to the eternal flames of hell. Here, therefore, are five verses of the Qur'an which are directly linked to the circumstances of the time, and concern exclusively the person of Abu Lahab and his wife.

When the Prophet led the Muslims to the battle of Tabuk, three of them remained behind without giving any reason and without asking permission from the Prophet. Later they repented, but the Muslims did not know this. They refused to frequent them or trade with them. The world seemed narrow and constricting to them. God came to their aid with this verse:

Likewise He pardoned the three who were left behind. Once the earth, so wide in expanse, had become constricted for them, and their very souls were constricted, and they came to believe that there can be no refuge from God except with Him, it was then that God turned towards them in pardon that they might turn to Him. It is God who is All-Pardoning, Compassionate to each.

(9:118) (Muqatil)³

According to 'A'isha:

– Glory to him who can hear everything!

Khawla bint Tha'laba came to see the Messenger of God and I overheard fragments of what she said to him, complaining of her spouse:

Messenger of God, he consumed my youth ... I offered my womb to him ... I grew older, I was no longer able to have children ... he spurned me ... I come to address my complaint to God ...

No sooner had she left that Gabriel came to communicate this verse:

God has heard the speech of the woman who disputed with you regarding her husband, as she complained to God, while God heard your conversation. God is All-Hearing, All-Seeing.

(58:1) (Al-Wahidi)⁴

131

Seventeen

Verses concerning historical events

Certain verses evoke specific historical events, and integrate historical time into the Word of God. Believers derive from these verses historical information or a moral message, but it is obvious that they cannot take them literally.

Persians and Byzantines were continuously at war. While the Prophet was still in Mecca, Khusru, the king of the Persians, inflicted a major defeat on the Byzantines. Caesar sent another army to the borders of Arabia to engage the Persians in battle, but it was also defeated.

The news reached Mecca, and was greeted with sadness by the Prophet and his companions, as the victory had been won by the Zoroastrians, people without scripture, over the Christians, people of the Book. The Quraysh [Meccan polytheists] on the other hand rejoiced. They went to see some companions of the Prophet and said:

– Our Persian brothers have defeated your Roman brothers [the Byzantines]. This is what will happen if you attack us, We shall vanquish you too.

God then revealed:

The Byzantines have been defeated in the nearer part of the land, and yet, after their defeat, they shall be the victorious – in a few years.

Abu Bakr, the closest companion of the Prophet, went to the Quraysh and said:

– Don't rejoice too quickly. In God's name, the Romans will defeat the Persians in a few years.

A member of the tribe of Quraysh replied:

– You are lying! Let us make a wager, with a time limit.

Abū Bakr wagered ten camels that the Romans would win in the space of three years. Then he went to see the Prophet and said:

– I have wagered with a member of Quraysh that the Almighty will give victory to the Romans within three years.

The Prophet replied:

– God said: in a few years. "A few" is between three and nine years. Go and see the member of Quraysh to increase the wager and lengthen the delay.

Abū Bakr went to see the man of Quraysh who said to him in an ironic tone:

– Have you come to change your mind?

– On the contrary. I have come to increase the wager and lengthen the time limit. Let us wager one hundred camels and increase the time limit to nine years.

– Agreed.

Before the time limit expired, they learned that the Romans had defeated the Persians.

(Qur'an, 30:2–4) (Muqatil)[1]

Not only is a particular war cited in the Qur'an, but it is also situated chronologically: "God said: **in a few years**". We may furthermore note that wagers and other games of chance will subsequently be forbidden by the Qur'an (5:90).

In the course of the last ten years of his life, the Prophet, who settled with his followers in Yathrib, commanded an army in several battles. Some of these battles are mentioned in the Qur'an, starting with the battle of Badr, which the Prophet won outright, even though the Meccan army was superior to that of the Muslims in men and equipment.

The armies of the Muslims and the Meccans faced one another before battle was joined. The Prophet, accompanied only by Abu Bakr, withdrew for a moment into the shelter which had been prepared for him. He implored God to grant him the victory he had been promised, saying:

– Lord, were your community to be vanquished on this day, there would be nobody to adore you!

Abu Bakr intervened:

– Messenger of God, you have no further need to

135

implore your Lord. It is sure that He will grant you the victory He has promised.

The Prophet suddenly experienced the sensation that accompanied God's revelations to him. Then he recovered and said:

– Let us rejoice, Abu Bakr! The victory of God is assured. The angel Gabriel has taken the reins of a horse covered in dust ...

God made Badr a decisive victory, mentioned in the Qur'an in these terms:

God gave you victory at Badr[2] when you were weak and small in number.

(3:123) (Ibn Ishaq)[3]

The battle of Hunayn was another memorable moment in the epic experience of the Prophet.

The Muslims numbered 11,500 against 4,000 warriors of the polytheist tribe of the Hawazin.

A Muslim said:

– We are in such a strong position compared to that of our enemy that we cannot be defeated.

After fierce fighting the polytheists felt they were defeated, but they plucked up their courage by repeating aloud while pointing to their women:

– Think of the humiliation of defeat! [The women would be sold as slaves and given to the men of the victorious side.]

They regained the upper hand and the Muslims, their line of battle broken, fell back in disorder. [The Prophet continued fighting, more and more isolated.] Al-'Abbas, paternal uncle of the Prophet, exhorted the Muslims to close ranks around the Prophet:

– You, the Ansar, allies of God and His Prophet! You, Muhajirun, who have sworn fidelity to the Prophet, it is the moment to come to his rescue!

The Muslims resumed fighting. A battalion of angels clad in white and mounted on alabaster-coloured horses, came to assist in their turn, until the polytheists were finally defeated.

The event is narrated thus in the Qur'an:

God gave you victory on many a battlefield. Recall the Day of Hunayn,[4] when you fancied your great number but it did not help you one whit ... you turned tail and fled. Then God made His serenity descend upon His Messenger and the believers, and sent down troops you did not see, and punished the unbelievers.

(9:25–6) (Muqatil)[5]

Several verses concern the battle of the Trench, in the course of which the Meccans, with a large tribal coalition, encircled Yathrib. The Prophet had had the time to have a trench dug around the city.

In the middle of the battle, some Muslims asked for permission to return home, saying that their houses were undefended.

It was then that a party of [the hypocrites] said: "People of Yathrib, this is no place for you to linger in, so fall back." And a group of them asked the Prophet's permission saying: "Our homes are totally exposed" – nor were they really exposed, for they merely intended to flee.

[In the end] God sent against the polytheists a cold wind, which uprooted the tent poles, extinguished campfires and frightened elephants, which fell on top of one another. Then the angels glorified in a loud voice the name of God over the heads of the polytheists, who abandoned the battle ...

God revealed:

O believers, remember the blessing of God upon you when enemy troops attacked you and We sent against them a wind, and troops invisible to you.

When the Muslims saw the enemy coalition falling back, they realised that God had kept the promise He had made to His Messenger.

When the believers saw the Confederates they said: "This is what God and His Messenger promised us, and God and His Messenger have spoken the truth." This only increased them in faith and submission.

(33:13, 9, 22) (Muqatil)[6]

ରୁ

In the light of these texts, it does not seem possible to see the Qur'an as a timeless book, completely detached from the historical context in which it was revealed. In its content and form, it is a dialogue between heaven and earth, in which God addresses, through His Prophet, the men and women of seventh-century Arabia. They wait, from day to day, for His Word to answer the many questions they were asking themselves, in order to attain a dwelling in Paradise in the next world, and an enhanced dignity in their lives on earth.

Eighteen

The abrogated verses

The question of the historical situation of the Qur'an becomes unavoidable as soon as we begin to discuss "abrogating verses" and "abrogated verses".

According to numerous chroniclers, this question was raised in the following context:

> The qibla was turned from Jerusalem to Mecca and the polytheists said:
>
> – How can Muhammad order his companions to do something that he subsequently forbids them, so as to order them to do something else? How can he say something today that he will retract tomorrow? Is the Qur'an merely the word of Muhammad, contradictory statements invented by him?

Then God revealed:

**For every verse We abrogate or cause to be forgotten,
We bring down one better or similar.**

(Qur'an, 2:106) (Al-Wahidi)[1]

Theologians and exegetes have continued to reflect throughout the centuries on the tenor and the consequences of this troubling verse.

But according to all the chroniclers, the abrogation of verses was considered at the time of the Prophet as an accepted practice. People alluded to it as a routine occurrence.

During morning prayer, the Prophet recited the sura:

Blessed is He Who sent down the Criterion upon His servant ...

At the moment when he greeted those assembled for prayer, he realised that he had omitted a verse. He asked:

– Is Ubayy present?

Ubayy answered:

– Yes.

– Why did you not remind me of the verse that I forgot?

– Messenger of God, I thought that it had been abrogated.

– No, it has not been abrogated.

(25:1) (Al-Baghdadi)[2]

'Ali ibn Abu Talib, a cousin of the Prophet, is said one day to have asked for a "recitation" of the Qur'an:
– Can you differentiate between the abrogating verses and the abrogated ones?
– No.
– Then you are damned and you condemn those who listen to you![3]

(Al-Harawi)[4]

Al-Suyuti even quotes a late source, according to which:

If the Prophet did not order all the verses of the Qur'an to be collected together in a single volume, it is because he expected some of them to be abrogated. When, on the death of the Prophet, Revelation ceased, God communicated to the inspired Caliphs the decision to collect the verses ...

(Rasm al-Mushaf)[5]

The majority of exegetical scholars agree on what is meant by abrogation: the operation by which God replaces one verse by another, revealed at a later date. There is a variety of possible different cases. In the first case (the least frequent), God can decree that everyone forget the abrogated verse.

It is recounted that one evening a believer wanted to recite a sura of the Qur'an, but was unable to do so. A second, then a third person wanted to recite it, but were unable to do so. The next day all three of them went to see the Prophet. The first said:

– Messenger of God, I wanted to recite this sura last night, but I was unable to do this.

The second said:

– I too was unable.

The third said:

– I too was unable.

Then the Prophet informed them:

– The sura was abrogated last night.

(Al Harawi)[6]

A second case: the abrogated verse can be removed from the Qur'an while remaining in people's memories. Some examples:

According to 'Asim ibn Bahdala:

Ibn Abu ibn Ka'b asked me:

– How many verses do you count in the sura of the Confederates [sura 33]?

– Seventy-three verses.

– Is that all? I saw that it contained as many verses as the sura of the Cow [286 verses].

(Mustafa Zayd)[7]

Anas ibn Malik recounts:

The seventy Ansar killed at Bi'r Ma'una were quoted in a verse as having said: "Tell our people that we have found our Lord, that he was satisfied with us and that he satisfied us." This verse was however abrogated.

(Mustafa Zayd)[8]

The third case is the most frequent: both the abrogated and the abrogating verses appear in the Qur'an. For example, the verse "**Wherever you turn, there is the Face of God**" (2:115) was abrogated by the verse: "**We have seen you turning your face from side to side in the heavens. So We will now turn you towards a direction that will please you: Turn your face towards the Sacred Mosque. Wherever you may be, turn your face towards it.**" (2:144)

There are numerous examples in the Qur'an of contradictory verses, which can only be explained if one verse abrogates the other. An essential problem is that of two Qur'anic verses, one of which has to replace the other. Which is the abrogating verse and which the abrogated? The answer is that one should know, relying on a precise source, which verse was revealed first. Here the texts concerned with *Asbab al-nuzūl* ("circumstances of the descent of the Qur'an") are invaluable, although even so doubts persist.

God revealed:
O Prophet, urge the believers on to the fight. If there are twenty steadfast among you they will overcome two hundred; if there are a hundred of you they will overcome a thousand unbelievers, for they are a people of

no understanding.

Hearing this, the Muslims were afraid. They found it unreasonable that twenty of them had to confront 200 infidels and that 100 Muslims had to confront 1,000 infidels. They shared these thoughts with the Prophet.

Then God revealed:

God has now lightened your burden, knowing that there is weakness in you. If there are a hundred of you, steadfast men, they will overcome two hundred, and if there are a thousand of you, they will overcome two thousand, by God's leave. God stands with the steadfast.
(8:65–6) (Al-Dahhak)[9]

When God turned the direction of the qibla from Jerusalem to Mecca, a group of Jews approached some Muslims and said to them:

– Tell us what we should think about praying while turned towards Jerusalem. When you prayed in this way were you following the path of righteousness or were you deluded? If it is the right way, why are you abandoning it? If you were deluded in the past, what is the fate of those who turned towards this qibla and died before its direction was changed? For many Muslims had died, who, while alive, had turned towards Jerusalem when praying.

The Muslims went to see the Prophet and said to him:

– The Almighty orders us to pray in the direction of Mecca. What is the fate of those of our brothers who are

146

dead, and prayed in the direction of Jerusalem?

God revealed:

We did not appoint the direction of prayer which you once followed, except to distinguish him who follows the Prophet from him who turns on his heels.

(2:143) (Al-Muqatil)[11]

One may note that this event, according to certain commentators, is linked to another event.

When the qibla was turned away from Jerusalem towards Mecca some Muslims abandoned Islam. At that point the Almighty revealed this verse.

(Al 'Asqalani)[12]

Now, let us quote again the verses relating to the marriage of the Prophet with Zaynab bint Jahsh:

Thus, when Zayd had satisfied his desire for her, We gave her in marriage to you in order that no blame might attach to the believers regarding wives of their adopted children, once they have satisfied their desire for them.

(33:37)

Then:

So call them [your adopted children] by their fathers' names: this is more fair with God.

Afterwards, Zayd was no longer designated the son of

147

nd adoption was forbidden in Islam.

(33:4) (Al Wahidi)[13]

renders adoption illegitimate, although it had
mitted by God for many years. What is **just in
s of God** has changed: adoption had hitherto been
ved, now it is rejected.

God revealed:

These shall be the nearest,
In the Gardens of Bliss,
A crowd of ancient communities,
And a few from latter times.

Hearing these verses, 'Umar ibn al Khattab wept. He said:

– Messenger of God, we believed in you, we followed you and, however, only a few of us will be saved!

Then God revealed:

A crowd of ancient communities,
And a crowd from latter times.

The Prophet had 'Umar brought to him and said:

– 'Umar, the Almighty has just revealed a verse in response to what you have said! He decrees: **A crowd of ancient communities, And a crowd from latter times.**

(56:13–4 and 39–40) (Al Wahidi)[14]

The principle of abrogation was one particularly relevant to the historical context in which the Prophet received the Revelation. The period during which the incipient Muslim community moved from Mecca to Yathrib was one of radical changes in the way the message of the Prophet took form: the attitude of Muslims towards the polytheists, as well as towards Christians and Jews, the relations between Muslims themselves, the way they understood the use of armed force: all these areas saw important changes. God defined the way that the message interacted with history as the prophetic mission of Muhammad unfolded. That is why God's word varied from period to period.

~

The theological implications of abrogation are so significant that in the twentieth century certain commentators suggested that the very notion of abrogation should be rejected as this entails recognising that the Qur'an contains a succession of historical moments, "befores and afters"; in other words, a temporal dimension. Thus, particular moments in which Revelation occurred can take on a special importance, while certain instances of Revelation replace others. All the verses of the Qur'an are not therefore unchangeable.

The imperative need to address the question of time in the Qur'an is one that causes difficulties for literalists, but there is no reason why it should cause difficulties for believers. Recognition of the temporal dimension of the Qur'an is in fact a way of recognising the plenitude of God's power and knowledge. It is because God intervenes in history that He can reveal truths that are relative and linked to a particular historical setting. When circumstances change, relative truths change with them. If there are two contradictory divine affirmations, this is because in the meantime truth has changed. God is always right at the time He speaks. But you have to situate each of His prescriptions in the context in which they were formulated: **"For every verse We abrogate or cause to be forgotten, We bring down one better or similar"** (2:106).

No verse can be "better" than another in the absolute. If one situates oneself in an absolute perspective, everything is of equal value and no comparison is possible. For a verse to be "better" than another, they must both be relative in their scope. They can both be true only if they relate to changing historical circumstances, and to changes which take place in time.

Nineteen

Circumstances and causes

Our priority in this book has been to show that an open-minded reading of the Qur'an, one that takes into account the circumstances of Revelation (*Asbab al-nuzul*), reveals a clear and simple truth: the Divine Word descended into human time.

How is it then that numerous exegetes, jurists and scholars, while continuing to refer to the study of *Asbab al-nuzul*, have not questioned literalist affirmations?

These scholars have accepted that the circumstances of Revelation may explain the background to the verses of the Qur'an, but do not cause the verses to take on a particular form. According to these scholars, the circumstances of the "descent" of the Qura'nic Revelation play no part in defining the content of these verses, in shaping them or in initiating their revelation. The form and the content of verses and the way in which they are revealed have as their sole cause the timeless Will of God which pre-exists the creation of the world. The context or circumstances of Revelation are part of creation and cannot be perceived as causes of Revelation.

How can one explain that these circumstances relate so closely to verses whose origin, creation and Revelation is purported to be independent of these same circumstances? If there is no relation of cause and effect between the Revelation and the circumstances of Revelation, how is it that the latter is so indispensable to the understanding of the former?

Scholars gave long consideration to these questions. Here are some examples of the answers they gave: a particular set of circumstances may "coincide" with the Revelation of a verse but this would only be an unnecessary "concomitance" between two distinct events. Another explanation was that God chose to create historical circumstances for the "descent" of eternal verses only to enable the believers to understand the verses. Such responses raise in turn new questions. The prayers, questions and expectations of the Prophet played an important part in the "descent" of a large part of the Qur'anic verses. Should one think that these intense experiences of the Prophet, recounted in the Hadith (words of the Prophet), were mere reflections of chance circumstances or mere pretexts chosen by God to reveal verses formulated before the Creation of the world?

On the other hand, how is it possible that certain

divinely revealed verses were subsequently abrogated by God, if these verses, which (according to scholars) participate in His eternal essence, are unaffected by historical processes?

Finally, how can one explain the people and events named in the text of the Qur'an, in other words, the traces of history in a timeless text?

We have seen how the Qur'an mentions events which occurred during the period of Revelation such as the battles of Badr, the Trench and Hunayn. In the Qur'an individuals are mentioned, contemporaries of the Prophet such as his adopted son, Zayd ibn Haritha, his blind companion, Ibn Umm Maktum, and the traitor, Abu Lahab, to say nothing of the Prophet himself, omnipresent in the Qur'an, whom God addresses directly and by name in order to reveal His Word.

If all the verses of the Qur'an were "uncreated" and were part – in their very formulation – of the timeless essence of God, a necessary consequence would be that all the persons and events evoked in the Qur'an would themselves be part of the eternal essence of God. These events are however part of the created world. How can this participate in the eternal essence of God? This would mean abolishing the ontological difference between God and his Creation, thus going against the teaching of the Qur'an.

The notion of the "uncreated" Qur'an thus leads to an impasse. It renders all the more clear and coherent the notion of the "created Qur'an", according to which the Word of God "descended" into Creation, revealing itself amid the changing circumstances of the preaching of the Prophet. If the historical context throws light on the meaning of numerous verses of the Qur'an, it is because this context is part of the temporal process of the Revelation of these verses.

Twenty

Yesterday and today

Having chosen the Arabs as the privileged recipients of his Word, God acted in such a way that the Word was fully revealed, and the majority of the main tribes of the Arabian Peninsula were united under the Prophet's authority, while he was still alive. After his death, the Arabs would be ready to pass on his message to the rest of humanity.

To this end God took charge of the earthly destiny of the incipient Muslim community, intervening in the many challenging situations faced by the Prophet during his preaching, responding to his appeals for help and guidance, resolving his dilemmas, coming to his aid, and all the while revealing the spiritual principle to which human minds and hearts could instantly open up.

In this way, contrary to Judaism and Christianity, rejected by the Arabs as too alien to their culture, the

Qur'an brought together the majority of the tribes of the Peninsula. God had crafted the Qur'an in such a way that it could penetrate the secret recesses of the hearts of the Arab and inspire believers to strive for spiritual solidarity which superseded tribal loyalties. Thus, Islam's innate tendency towards unity prevailed over the divisions that characterise tribal society.

ભ

During the twenty-two years of Revelation, what was the experience of the Prophet's companions?

The branch of exegesis known as *Asbab al-nuzul* provides us with some essential elements which help to answer this question. It enables us to understand not only the Qur'an, but also the mentality of those who lived at the period of the Revelation of the Qur'an. This element takes on, with good reason, an exemplary value for all Muslims. The first believers, who rallied round the Prophet and faced every kind of danger at his side, while waiting for the "descent" of the verses of the Qur'an, represent the Muslim par excellence. They are the bearers of an irreplaceable message for those who follow them.

This is why the image which is projected of the first Muslim community, and in particular the way in which it lived out its relationship with God, is so important. It naturally conditions the attitude of believers today.

The most common image which prevails today is that of a community of men and women passively waiting for an inaccessible God to reveal commandments which cannot be altered.

The *Asbab al-nuzul* presents a very different picture: one of men and women who constantly felt that they were close to an all-powerful God, one full of compassion and generosity. They addressed Him through his Prophet, with a freedom and frankness which reflected their faith. Throughout these crucial years they played a fully responsible role in the unfolding history of their community.

They received from God the basis of the "true religion" as well as the various prescriptions regulating their life on earth, entrusting themselves to His will. They nevertheless were able to express themselves; they did so, believing that they had the right to address God and that He would listen to them.

The believing community thus interiorised the commandments of God in a spirit of veneration and obedience, but also by sincerity, energy, and even vehemence on the part of men and women whose existence was opening on to a new horizon, and who had developed, thanks to the divine message, self-awareness and a sense of responsibility.

The Companions of the Prophet thus spoke to the Prophet in varying ways. For instance, precise questions were addressed to the Prophet, with the expectation of a reply:

The Muslims were returning home after the conclusion of the truce of Al-Hudaybiyya, sad and dejected at not having been able to accomplish the pilgrimage for which they had set out. At this point the Almighty revealed to His Messenger:

We have granted you a conspicuous victory,

That God may forgive your sins, past and to come,

And complete His favour upon you,

And guide you to a straight path,

And lend you His mighty aid.

When the Messenger of God recited this verse to his companions, one of them said:

– Messenger of God, we should be pleased with what the Almighty has prepared for you and granted to you. What has He prepared for us and what shall He grant to us?

The Almighty then revealed:

Give glad tidings to the believers that they shall obtain from God a marvellous favour.

And:

He will admit the believers, male and female, into Gardens beneath which rivers flow, abiding therein for ever, and He shall pardon their sins – this is the greatest triumph in God's sight.

(Qur'an, 48:1–2, 33:47, 48:5) (Muqatil)[1] (Al-Wahidi)[2]

Believers could also request, with a degree of insistence, clarifications and details:

'Umar ibn al-Khattab asked openly:

– Lord, tell us what we should think about wine!

The Messenger of God recited the following verse to him:

They ask you about wine and gambling.

Say: "In them both lies grave sin, though some benefit, to mankind. But their sin is more grave than their benefit."

'Abd al-Rahman ibn 'Awf prepared a meal to which he invited several of the companions of the Messenger of God. They ate food and drank wine.

When the time for evening prayer came, he wanted to lead his companions in prayer and he said:

– Say: O you the unbelievers ...

He was unable to continue.

On learning this 'Umar again spoke up:

– Lord, guide us with an explicit verse on wine!

Then God revealed another verse:

O believers, do not come near to prayer when you are drunk, unless you know what you are saying ...

However, the uncle of the Prophet, while drunk, savagely killed two camels belonging to his nephew 'Ali. When the Prophet went to reproach him, his uncle greeted him with insults. Irritated by this, 'Umar requested a verse on the subject of wine which was more intransigent in character.

Then God revealed this third verse:

O believers, wine and gambling, idols and divining arrows are an abhorrence, the work of Satan. So keep away from it, that you may prevail.

(2:219, 4:43, 5:90) (Al Harawi)[3]

Muslims could go even further, objecting to certain verses which seemed too demanding or whose effects were directly damaging to them:

God revealed:

Whether you reveal what lies in your souls or whether you conceal it, God will hold you to account, forgiving whomever He wills and punishing whomever He wills.

The Muslims no longer knew what to do. Abu Bakr, 'Umar, and other companions came to see the Messenger of God, knelt before him, and said:

– Messenger of God, the Almighty commands us to fulfil as best we can the obligations of prayer, fasting, combat in defence of Islam and almsgiving. The most recently revealed verse is beyond us. We have never heard such a harsh verse. We often have thoughts that we subsequently banish from our hearts. The world is full of temptations. Does God wish to punish us for each of the thoughts that occur to us? We shall all be condemned to hell.

The Messenger of God answered:

– Thus was the verse revealed to me.

– In this case we are all condemned, because what is commanded is too much for us. (...)

They went away, more and more anxious. Then God came to their help and revealed:

God charges not any soul except with what it can bear. To its credit belongs what it has earned: upon it falls the burden of what it has deserved.

This verse abrogated the preceding verse. The Messenger of God said:

– In the case of my people, God closes His eyes to the thoughts of each person as long as these thoughts have not been expressed in actions and words.

(2:284, 286) (Al-Wahidi)[4] (al Harawi)[5]

God revealed:

And the poets – the tempters follow them.
Do you not see how they wander in every valley,
Boasting of things they have not done?

There were, however, Muslim poets who put the words of the Prophet in verse. Bedouin tribesmen listened to these verses and recited them in their turn. Some of these poets went to see the Prophet and objected to these verses:

– We are damned.

Then God revealed these verses:

Except for those who believe and do good deeds,
Who mention the name of God often ...

(26:224–6, 227) (Al Mawardi)[6]

☙

The companions of the Prophet lived out in a profound manner the verses of the Qur'an, making its message and meaning their own. Thus they felt entitled to ask God to modify verses which seemed too far removed from their existential landmarks, or which troubled their conscience.

If such was the mood of the first Muslims at the particular historical moment when the divine Revelation occurred, how can one claim, fourteen centuries later, that all the verses of the Qur'an should be followed exactly as they are, word for word?

Since the time of the Revelation of the Qur'an, we have not only moved on from a particular historical period to another one, but we inhabit a different world altogether. Our mental categories, technical references and individual priorities have nothing to do with those of the people who lived at the time of the Qur'anic Revelation. The different religions, communities and cultures together form a single humanity. Their individual destinies, albeit contradictory, are inseparable from one another. Thus, relations between Muslims and non-Muslims, believers and non-believers, the spiritual and the temporal, individuals and communities have taken forms that would have been unimaginable for the first generation of Muslims.

Today, therefore, it is meaningless to follow to the letter verses calling for the freeing of a slave in order to gain pardon for one's sins. Now that slavery has officially disappeared in Muslim countries, one cannot re-establish it so as to obtain pardon through the liberation of slaves. It is equally meaningless to follow literally verses which put women in an inferior social situation. At a time when women go to school and university, work in factories and offices, and take up posts at the highest levels of responsibility, it is impossible to deny them full civic equality on the grounds that the social position to which they acceded at the time of the Revelation of the Qur'an was higher than that which they enjoyed in Arab polytheist society.

Meaningless, too, are the verses which call on believers to defend Islam by the sword. Nowhere today – including in non-Muslim countries – are Muslims prevented from freely and openly preaching: it is therefore impossible to accord believers of other religious faiths the same treatment as that accorded to the polytheists who expelled the Prophet from Mecca.

Most Muslim countries have abolished slavery. They have granted women voting rights and eligibility for office on an equal footing to men. They have ratified the Charter of the United Nations, in virtue of which they peacefully cooperate with peoples who do not possess any religious belief. Thus they contravene several Qu'ranic prescriptions. This does not mean they have renounced the Qur'an. They have recognised, practically if not legally, that the provisions of the Qur'an do not all have the same validity and that some of them, marked by their original historical context, are no longer relevant to the contemporary world.

CR

In today's world, following the example of the companions of the Prophet means taking a course contrary to that which the literalists urge us to follow. It means recognising that Qur'anic prescriptions, which reflect the specific aspirations of people in the seventh century, can no longer guide men and women in the twenty-first century.

Thus believers are relieved of a crushing burden, one that involves cheating one's conscience, ignoring or skirting round certain Qu'ranic prescriptions while believing that one has to follow them. They recover their interior freedom and are open to the spiritual and human adventure to which believers are invited by the Qur'an.

This means not summing up the world in the Qur'an, but instead discovering the world, guided by the message of the Qur'an, and seeking the path of God among the many paths of life. Believers will thus discover ever more distant depths, wider horizons and more subtle echoes amid the myriad dimensions of meaning that God gives His creation.

Thus they can take up the mission with which God has invested them, that of doing **"righteous deeds to make them inherit the earth"** (24:55).

In order to do this, they have a mission to carry out for the benefit of their fellow men, as well as duties towards God that they are required to carry out.

Virtue does not demand of you to turn your faces east-
wards or westwards. Virtue rather is:

He who believes in God, the Last Day, the angels, the
Book and the prophets;

Who dispenses money, though dear, to kinsmen,
orphans, the needy, the traveller, beggars and for
ransom;

Who performs the prayer and pays the alms;

Who fulfils their contracts when they contract;

Who are steadfast in hardship, calamity and danger;

These are the true believers.

These are truly pious.

(2:177)

As for ritual obligations, they are clearly and simply laid
out, and every believer is capable of carrying them out:

A man belonging to a Bedouin tribe came to see the
Messenger of God and questioned him:

– One of your emissaries says that you are the Messenger
of God.

The Messenger of God confirmed this ...

The man then asked:

– Your emissary says that we have to pray five times
throughout the day.

– The emissary has spoken the truth.

– In the name of He who sends you, it is really God who
commands this?

– Yes.

– Your emissary says, we have to give a proportion of our property as alms.

– The emissary has spoken the truth.

– In the name of He who sends you, it is really God who commands this?

– Yes.

– Your emissary says that we have to fast during the month of Ramadan.

– The emissary has spoken the truth.

– In the name of He who sends you, it is really God who commands this?

– Yes.

– Your emissary says that the pilgrimage to Mecca is obligatory for those who can accomplish it.

– The emissary has spoken the truth.

– In the name of He who sends you with the Truth, I shall do no more and no less than this.

When he had gone the Prophet said to those around him:

– If he does what he says he will go to Paradise.

(Muslim[7])

[After the death of the Prophet] 'Abd Allah, son of 'Umar ibn al-Khattab, answered in this way to a man who asked him why he took no part in war:

– I heard the Prophet of God say: Islam is based on five pillars: the affirmation that there is no God but God,

166

prayer, alms-giving, the Ramadan fast and the pilgrimage
to the House of God.

(Muslim[8])

Beyond faith in God and observance of the ritual duties
which He commands, believers are called to act on earth
in a way directed towards the wellbeing of fellow men and
women. The light of the Qur'an illuminates the spiritual
and moral dimensions of their journey, while leaving to
the individual the freedom to choose how to behave. Each
person has to make these choices in accordance with his
or her own conscience, for he or she will be held fully
responsible on the Day of Judgement.

Notes

Chapter 1

1. Hussein, *Al Sira. Le Prophète de l'islam raconté par ses compagnons*, 2 vols (Paris: Grasset, 2005–2007).
2. *The Qur'an: A New Translation by Tarif Khalidi* (New York: Penguin Classics, 2008). All Qur'anic verses are taken from this translation and are referenced as sura:aya (chapter number:verse number).

Chapter 2

1. Ibn Tamiyya was an *alim* (theologian and scholar) from Syria who specialised in Jurisprudence and followed the Ibn Hanbal school of Law.
2. Muhammad ibn Abd al-Wahhab was a Salafi theologian from the Najd region of Saudi Arabia. He founded the Wahhabi school of thought and in a pact with Muhammad ibn Saud established the first Saudi State.

Chapter 5

1. Ibn Ishaq, *Al-Sira al-Nabawiyya*, ed. Ibn Hisham (Dar al-Jil: Beirut, 1975), vol. 1, p. 119.
2. Ibn Sa'd, *Kitab al-Tabaqat al-Kabir*, prepared by 'Ali Muhammad 'Umar (Maktabat al-Khanji: Cairo, 2001), vol. 1, p. 165.
3. Al-Tabari, *Tarikh al-Rusul wa al-Muluk* (Dar al-Ma'arif: Cairo, 1970), p. 298.
4. Al-Wahidi, *Asbab Nuzul al-Qur'an* (Dar al-Kutub al-'ilmiyya:

Beirut, 1998), p. 15.

5. Al-Mawardi, *Tafsir* (Dar al-Kutub al-'ilmiyya: Beirut, 1992), p. 135.

6. *Kitab al-Tabaqat al-Kabir*, vol. 1, p. 167.

7. *Asbab Nuzul al-Qur'an*, p. 481.

8. Al-Dhahabi, *Siyar a'lam al-nubala'* (Mu'asasat al-Risala: Beirut, 1997), vol. 1, p. 117.

Chapter 8

1. Al-Bukhari, *Sahih* ["Authentic Hadith"], Maktabat al-Thawafa al-'arabiyya: Cairo, 2001, Hadith 5002, p.608.

Chapter 9

1. Al-Zamakhshari, *Tafsir* (Dar al-Ma'rifa: Beirut, 2005), p. 650.

2. *Asbab Nuzul al-Qur'an*, p. 312.

3. Ibid. p. 501.

4. Al-Zamakhshari, *Tafsir* (Dar al-Ma'rifa: Beirut, 2005), p. 745.

5. Ibid. p. 325.

6. Al-Wahidi, *Asbab Nuzul al-Qur'an* (Dar al-Kutub al-'ilmiyya: Beirut, 1998), p. 205.

7. The most powerful tribal coalition in Mecca.

8. Abu Talib's support had been decisive for the survival of the small Muslim community at the beginning of its history.

9. *Asbab Nuzul al-Qur'an*, p. 266.

10. Ibn Ishaq, *Al-Sira al-Nabawiyya*, ed. Ibn Hisham (Dar al-Jil: Beirut, 1975), p. 216.

11. *Al-Sira al-Nabawiyya*, p. 263.

12. Al-Zamakhshari, *Tafsir* (Dar al-Ma'rifa: Beirut, 2005) p. 584.

13. Ibn Kathir, *Al-bidaya wa al-Nihaya* (Dar ihya al-Turath al-'arabi: Beirut), vol. 3, p. 68.

14. Maqatil, *Tafsir* (Dar al-Kutub al-'ilmiyya: Beirut, 2003), p. 272.

15. Al-Wahidi, *Asbab Nuzul al-Qur'an* (Dar al-Kutub al-'ilmiyya: Beirut, 1998), p. 300.

16. Ibid. p. 232.

17. *Tafsir*, p. 573.

Chapter 10

1. Al-Wahidi, *Asbab Nuzul al-Qur'an* (Dar al-Kutub al-'ilmiyya: Beirut, 1998), p. 170.

Chapter 11

1. Muslims are those who "surrender themselves to God".
2. The Sabeans were an ancient Near Eastern religious community considered by the Qur'an to belong to the People of the Book (Ahl al-Kitab) – people to whom a divine scripture had been revealed (see Tarif Khalidi's translation, p. 529).
3. Al-'Asqalani, *Al-i'jab fi bayan al-asbab* (Dar Ibn Hazm: Beirut, 2002), p. 90.
4. Ibn Ishaq, *Al-Sira al-Nabawiyya*, ed. Ibn Hisham (Dar al-Jil: Beirut, 1975), vol. 2, p. 143.
5. *Al-i'jab fi bayan al-asab*, p. 123.
6. Al-Wahidi, *Asbab Nuzul al-Qur'an* (Dar al-Kutub al-'ilmiyya: Beirut, 1998), p. 394.
7. Ibid. p. 386.
8. Al-Zamakhshari, *Tafsir* (Dar al-Ma'rifa: Beirut, 2005), p. 983.
9. *Asbab Nuzul al-Qur'an*, p. 390.
10. *Asbab Nuzul al-Qur'an*, p. 414.
11. Maqatil, *Tafsir* (Dar al-Kutub al-'ilmiyya: Beirut, 2003), vol. 1, p. 268.
12. *Tafsir*, p. 268.
13. *Asbab Nuzul al-Qur'an*, p. 280.

Chapter 12

1. Ibn Ishaq, *Al-Sira al-Nabawiyya*, ed. Ibn Hisham (Dar al-Jil: Beirut, 1975), vol. 2, p. 144.
2. Ibid. p. 141.
3. Al-Wahidi, *Asbab Nuzul al-Qur'an* (Dar al-Kutub al-'ilmiyya: Beirut, 1998), p. 106.
4. *Al-Sira al-Nabawiyya*, vol. 2, p. 160.

Chapter 13
1. Muslims from Mecca who had emigrated to Yathrib.
2. Inhabitants of Yathrib who had converted to Islam.
3. Al-Wahidi, *Asbab Nuzul al-Qur'an* (Dar al-Kutub al-'ilmiyya: Beirut, 1998), p. 411.
4. Al-Zamakhshari, *Tafsir* (Dar al-Ma'rifa: Beirut, 2005), p. 104.
5. *Asbab Nuzul al-Qur'an*, p. 370.
6. Maqatil, *Tafsir* (Dar al-Kutub al-'ilmiyya: Beirut, 2003), vol. 3, p. 46.
7. Ibid. vol. I, p. 97.
8. *Asbab Nuzul al-Qur'an*, p. 158.
9. Ibid. p. 158.
10. *Tafsir*, vol. 1, p. 317.
11. *Asbab Nuzul al-Qur'an*, p. 208.
12. Ibid. p. 55.
13. Ibid. p. 274.
14. *Tafsir*, p. 1105.
15. *Asbab Nuzul al-Qur'an*, p. 448.
16. Ibid. p. 69.
17. Ibid. p. 377.
18. Ibid. p. 150.
19. *Tafsir*, vol. 1, p. 274.
20. *Asbab Nuzul al-Qur'an*, p. 155.
21. *Tafsir*, p. 235.

Chapter 14
1. Al-Wahidi, *Asbab Nuzul al-Qur'an* (Dar al-Kutub al-'ilmiyya: Beirut, 1998), p. 471.
2. Al-Zamakhshari, *Tafsir* (Dar al-Ma'rifa: Beirut, 2005), p. 179.
3. Maqatil, *Tafsir*, Dar al-Kutub al-'ilmiyya: Beirut, 2003), vol. 1, p. 248.
4. *Tafsir*, p. 229.
5. *Asbab Nuzul al-Qur'an*, p. 471.
6. *Tafsir*, p. 102.
7. Ibn Ishaq, *Al-Sira al-Nabawiyya*, ed. Ibn Hisham (Dar al-Jil:

Beirut, 1975), vol. 2, p. 143.

8. *Asbab Nuzul al-Qur'an*, p. 389.

9. Ibid. p. 289.

10. *Tafsir*, vol. 2, p. 244.

11. *Tafsir*, p. 1039.

12. Ibid. p. 596.

13. *Asbab Nuzul al-Qur'an*, p. 276.

14. *Tafsir*, p. 604.

15. A Coptic slave by whom the Prophet had a son who died shortly after being born to him.

16. *Asbab Nuzul al-Qur'an*, p. 460.

17. *Tafsir*, p. 1119.

18. *Asbab Nuzul al-Qur'an*, p. 283.

19. *Asbab Nuzul al-Qur'an*, p. 261.

20. Ibid. p. 582.

21. *Tafsir*, vol. 1, p. 324.

22. Ibid. vol. 3, p. 47.

23. Ibn Sa'd, *Kitab al-Tabaqat al-Kabir*, prepared by 'Ali Muhammad 'Umar (Maktabat al-Khanji: Cairo, 2001), vol. 10, p. 105.

Chapter 15

1. Al-Wahidi, *Asbab Nuzul al-Qur'an* (Dar al-Kutub al-'ilmiyya: Beirut, 1998), p. 403.

2. Al-Zamakhshari, *Tafsir* (Dar al-Ma'rifa: Beirut, 2005), p. 1034.

3. *Asbab Nuzul al-Qur'an*, p. 402.

4. Ibid. p. 354.

5. *Tafsir*, p. 863.

6. *Tafsir*, p. 862.

Chapter 16

1. The Prophet's uncle and enemy.

2. Ibn Kathir, *Al-bidaya wa al-Nihaya* (Dar ihya al-Turath al-'arabi: Beirut), vol. 3, p. 53.

3. Maqatil, *Tafsir* (Dar al-Kutub al-'ilmiyya: Beirut, 2003), vol. 2, p. 75.

4. Al-Wahidi, *Asbab Nuzul al-Qur'an* (Dar al-Kutub al-'ilmiyya: Beirut, 1998), p. 427.

Chapter 17

1. Maqatil, *Tafsir* (Dar al-Kutub al-'ilmiyya: Beirut, 2003), vol. 3, p. 3.
2. A well south-west of Medina, site of the first major Muslim victory over the Meccans (the battle of Badr, 624).
3. Ibn Ishaq, *Al-Sira al-Nabawiyya*, ed. Ibn Hisham (Dar al-Jil: Beirut, 1975), vol. 2, p. 196.
4. A valley near Mecca, site of a fierce battle in 630, resulting in a Muslim victory.
5. *Tafsir*, vol. 2, p. 41.
6. *Tafsir*, vol. 3, pp. 37–9.

Chapter 20

1. Maqatil, *Tafsir* (Dar al-Kutub al-'ilmiyya: Beirut, 2003), vol. 3, p. 245.
2. Al-Wahidi, *Asbab Nuzul al-Qur'an* (Dar al-Kutub al-'ilmiyya: Beirut, 1998), p. 398.
3. Al-Harawi, *Al-Nasikh wa al-Mansukh fi al-Qur'an al-'Aziz* (Maktabat al-Rushd: Riyad, 1997), p. 249.
4. *Asbab Nuzul al-Qur'an*, p. 97.
5. *Al-Nasikh wa al-Mansukh fi al-Qur'an al-'Aziz,* p. 275.
6. Al-Mawardi, *Tafsir* (Dar al-Kutub al-'ilmiyya: Beirut, 1992), vol. 4, p. 190.
7. Muslim, *Sahih* (Maktabat al-Thaqafa al-'arabiyya: Cairo, 2004), p. 17.
8. *Sahih*, p. 18.

Chapter 18

1. Al-Wahidi, *Asbab Nuzul al-Qur'an*, Dar al-Kutub al-'ilmiyya: Beirut, 1998, p. 37.
2. Al-Baghdadi, *Al-asma' al-mubhama fi al-anba' al-'muhkama* (Maktabat al-Khanji: Cairo, 1997), p. 12.

3. This is because he attributes to God verses of which certain have been abrogated and, therefore, are no longer valid.

4. Al-Harawi, *Al-Nasikh wa al-Mansukh fi al-Qur'an al-'Aziz* (Maktabat al-Rushd: Riyad, 1997), p. 4.

5. Ghanim Qadduri al-Hamad, *Rasm al-Mushaf* (Beirut: Mu'assasat al-Matbu'at al-'arabiyya, 1982), p. 99.

6. *Al-Nasikh wa al-Mansukh fi al-Qur'an al-'Aziz*, p. 15.

7. Mustafa Zayd, *Al Naskh fi al-Qur'an al-Karim* (Dar al-wafa': Mansoura, 1987), vol. 1, p. 285.

8. Ibid. vol. 1, p. 281.

9. Al-Dahhak, *Tafsir* (Dar al-Salam: Cairo, 1999), p. 395.

10. He did this by abrogating the verse indicating the first direction of prayer, and replacing it by the verse indicating the new direction.

11. Maqatil, *Tafsir* (Dar al-Kutub al-'ilmiyya: Beirut, 2003), vol. 1, p. 84.

12. Al-'Asqalani, *Al-i'jab fi bayan al-asbab* (Dar Ibn Hazm: Beirut, 2002), p. 211.

13. *Asbab Nuzul al-Qur'an*, p. 365.

14. Ibid. p. 422.

Works cited

Al-'Asqalani, *Al-i'jab fi bayan al-asbab* ["Book of genealogy"], Dar Ibn Hazm: Beirut, 2002.

Al-Baghdadi, *Al-asma' al-mubhama fi al-anba' al-'muhkama* ["Identifying unnamed individuals mentioned in Hadith"], Maktabat al-Khanji: Cairo, 1997.

Al-Bukhari, *Sahih* ["Authentic Hadith"], Maktabat al-Thawafa al-'arabiyya: Cairo, 2001.

Al-Dahhak, *Tafsir* ["Commentary"], Dar al-Salam: Cairo, 1999.

Al-Dhahabi, *Siyar a'lam al-nubala'* ["The life of noble figures"], Mu'asasat al-Risala: Beirut, 1997.

Al-Harawi, *Al-Nasikh wa al-Mansukh fi al-Qur'an al-'Aziz* ["The abrogator and the abrogated in the Holy Qur'an"], Maktabat al-Rushd: Riyad, 1997.

Al-Mawardi, *Tafsir* ["Commentary"], Dar al-Kutub al-'ilmiyya: Beirut, 1992.

Al-Suyuti, *Al-Jami'al Saghir* ["The minor collection and its addenda"], Damas, 1997.

Al-Tabari, *Tarikh al-Rusul wa al-Muluk* ["The history of the Prophets and Kings"], Dar al-Ma'arif: Cairo, 1970.

Al-Wahidi, *Asbab Nuzul al-Qur'an* ["Circumstances of the descent of the Qur'an"], Dar al-Kutub al-'ilmiyya: Beirut, 1998.

Al-Zamakhshari, *Tafsir* ["Commentary"], Dar al-Ma'rifa: Beirut, 2005.

Ibn Baskhawal, *Al-Ghawamid wa al-Mubhamat* ["Uncertainties and ambiguities"], Dar al-Andalus al-Khadra: Jeddah, 1994.

Ibn Ishaq, *Al-Sira al-Nabawiyya* ["The life of the Prophet Muhammad"], ed. Ibn Hisham, Dar al-Jil: Beirut, 1975.

Ibn Kathir, *Al-bidaya wa al-Nihaya* ["The beginning and the end"], Dar ihya al-Turath al-'arabi: Beirut.

Ibn Sa'd, *Kitab al-Tabaqat al-Kabir* ["The book of the circles of companions"], prepared by 'Ali Muhammad 'Umar, Maktabat al-Khanji: Cairo, 2001.

Muqatil, *Tafsir* ["Commentary"], Dar al-Kutub al-'ilmiyya: Beirut, 2003.

Muslim, *Sahih* ["Authentic Hadith"], Maktabat al-Thaqafa al-'arabiyya: Cairo, 2004.

Zayd, Mustafa, *Al Naskh fi al-Qur'an al-Karim* ["Abrogation in the Holy Qur'an"], Dar al-wafa': Mansoura, 1987.